VEGETARIAN
COOK BOOK

VEGETARIAN
COOK BOOK

k

Published by
Kandour Ltd
1-3 Colebrooke Place
London N1 8HZ

This edition published 2005

This edition printed in 2005 for
Bookmart Ltd
Registered Number 2372865
Trading As Bookmart Ltd
Blaby Road
Wigston
Leicester
LE18 4SE

Title: Vegetarian Cook Book

Editorial and design management: Metro Media
Author: Victoria Worsley
Design/layout: Lee Coventry
Original design concept: Christine Fent
Photography: photos.com

Printed and bound in India

ISBN 1-904756-35-2

CONTENTS

CONTENTS

INTRODUCTION

People begin following a vegetarian diet for many reasons and in recent years it has become ever more popular and easy to do so, with all restaurants featuring vegetarian dishes and supermarkets displaying a large range of meat-free products. So, whatever your reasons, be they religious reasons, health reasons or because you don't like the idea of eating animals, there is now no reason not to have an interesting and balanced vegetarian diet.

And if you're entertaining friends or business colleagues, a vegetarian menu is guaranteed not to offend anyone's beliefs. This cook book provides everything you need to offer a vegetarian menu to suit any occasion, however formal. Soups, starters and salads, pastas, grains and main courses – all are here. We decided to pack the book full of delicious meat-free main dishes, as it is usually easy to find a vegetarian dessert.

So, there is something for everyone here, including vegetarian versions of classic meat dishes. There's plenty to try and new family favourites just waiting to be discovered.

SOUPS

A great way to start a sit-down dinner, soups have been around for years and years and remain very popular. And even without meat, the variations are endless. Here there is a range between the traditional and the more exotic, with ingredients including peanuts, ginger, melon, Stilton and chickpeas, as well as the more usual tomatoes, parsnips, carrots and onions.

Soups are also great for lunch time or when you're feeling under the weather. Chicken soup is a famous comfort food, but here the meat is replaced by healthy fruits and vegetables in combinations such as leek and potato, or apple and sweet potato.

ONION SOUP

Serves 4

INGREDIENTS
450g/1lb onions, diced
1 garlic clove, crushed
75g/3oz butter
50g/2oz plain flour
600ml/1pt vegetable stock
600ml/1pt milk
3 tsp lemon juice
1 bay leaf
1 carrot, grated
4 tbsp double cream
Salt and pepper

In a saucepan over a low heat, fry the onions and garlic in the butter, stirring frequently, until soft. Stir in the flour and cook, stirring, for a further 1 minute. Gradually stir in the stock and bring to the boil, stirring frequently. Add the milk, then bring back to the boil.

Add the lemon juice and bay leaf. Cover and simmer for 25 minutes until the vegetables are tender. Discard the bay leaf. Stir in the carrot and simmer for 3 minutes. Stir in the cream and reheat. Season to taste before serving.

WATERCRESS SOUP

Serves 6

INGREDIENTS
6 spring onions, chopped
1/2 onion, chopped
400g/14oz watercress, roughly chopped
100g/4oz butter
50g/2oz plain flour
750ml/1 1/4pts vegetable stock
300ml/1/2pt water
Salt and pepper

In a large pan, cook the spring onions, onion and watercress in the butter over a low heat for 3 minutes. Add the flour and stir until combined.

Gradually add the stock and water and stir well until smooth. Bring to the boil, then reduce the heat and simmer, covered, for 10 minutes. Leave to cool slightly.

Transfer the mixture to a blender or food processor and process until smooth. Gently reheat and season before serving.

CHICKPEA SOUP

Serves 4

INGREDIENTS
2 tbsp olive oil
2 leeks, sliced
2 courgettes, diced
2 garlic cloves, crushed
800g/1lb 12oz canned chopped tomatoes
1 tbsp tomato purée
1 bay leaf
850ml/1 1/2pts vegetable stock
400g/14oz canned chickpeas, drained
Salt and pepper

Heat the oil in a large saucepan, add the leek and courgettes and cook, stirring constantly, for 5 minutes. Add the garlic, tomatoes, tomato purée, bay leaf, stock and chickpeas and stir well. Bring to the boil, reduce the heat and simmer for 5 minutes.

Season to taste and discard the bay leaf. Serve immediately.

CARROT AND GINGER SOUP

Serves 4

INGREDIENTS
2 tsp olive oil
1 onion, chopped
1 garlic clove, peeled and crushed
1/2 tsp ground ginger
450g/1lb carrots, chopped
1.2 litres/2pts vegetable stock
2.5cm/1in piece fresh root ginger, peeled and grated
Salt and pepper
1 tbsp lemon juice

Heat the oil in a large saucepan and gently cook the onion and garlic for 4 minutes. Stir in the ground ginger and cook for a further 1 minute. Add the carrots, stock and fresh ginger and simmer gently for 15 minutes.

Transfer to a blender or food processor and purée until smooth, then season to taste. Stir in the lemon juice and serve immediately.

CHEESE AND WALNUT SOUP

Serves 4

INGREDIENTS
50g/2oz butter
1 garlic clove, crushed
2 shallots, chopped
3 celery stalks, chopped
2 tbsp plain flour
300ml/1/2pt milk
600ml/1pt vegetable stock
150g/5oz blue Stilton cheese, crumbled
2 tbsp chopped walnut halves
150ml/1/4pt natural yogurt
Salt and pepper

Melt the butter in a large saucepan and cook the garlic, shallots and celery until they are softened. Reduce the heat, add the flour and stir for 30 seconds. Add the milk and stock and bring to the boil.

Lower the heat, add the Stilton and walnuts, then cover and simmer for 20 minutes.

Stir in the yogurt and heat through, then season to taste before serving.

PEANUT SOUP

Serves 6

INGREDIENTS
2 tbsp olive oil
1 onion, finely chopped
2 garlic cloves, crushed
1 tsp mild chilli powder
2 red peppers, finely chopped
225g/8oz carrots, finely chopped
3 celery stalks, sliced
225g/8oz potatoes, finely chopped
900ml/1 1/2pts vegetable stock
6 tbsp crunchy peanut butter
Salt and pepper
2 tbsp crushed salted peanuts

Heat the oil in a large saucepan and cook the onion and garlic until soft, stirring occasionally. Stir in the chilli powder and cook for a further 1 minute.

Add the peppers, carrots, celery and potatoes and cook for 4 minutes, stirring occasionally. Add the stock and peanut butter and stir well until combined. Season to taste.

Bring to the boil, then reduce the heat, cover and simmer for 20 minutes. Adjust the seasoning and serve garnished with the peanuts.

APPLE AND SWEET POTATO SOUP

Serves 6

INGREDIENTS
1 tbsp butter
3 leeks, thinly sliced
2 large Bramley apples, peeled and diced
600g/1lb 5oz sweet potatoes, peeled and diced
1.2 litres/2pts vegetable stock
Salt and pepper
225ml/8fl oz apple juice
225ml/8fl oz single cream

Melt the butter in a large saucepan, then add the leeks. Cover and cook over a medium-low heat for 7 minutes, stirring frequently. Add the apples, sweet potatoes and stock, then season to taste.

Bring to the boil, then reduce the heat and simmer, covered, for 20 minutes. Leave to cool slightly, then transfer to a blender or food processor and process until smooth.

Return the soup to the pan and stir in the apple juice. Place over a low heat and simmer for 10 minutes. Stir in the cream and simmer for a further 5 minutes, until heated through.

PARMESAN AND CAULIFLOWER SOUP

Serves 6

INGREDIENTS
1.2 litres/2pts vegetable stock
1 large cauliflower, cut into florets
175g/6oz farfalle
150ml/¼pt single cream
50g/2oz Parmesan cheese, grated
Salt and pepper

Bring the stock to the boil in a large saucepan. Add the cauliflower and simmer for 10 minutes. Remove the cauliflower and place in a blender or food processor.

Add the farfalle to the stock and simmer for 10 minutes. Drain and add the stock to the cauliflower in the blender or food processor, then add the cream. Blend until smooth and pour into a clean pan. Stir in the farfalle and then reheat, stirring occasionally. Stir in the Parmesan and heat through. Season to taste before serving.

SPICY PARSNIP SOUP

Serves 4

INGREDIENTS
1 tsp olive oil
1 onion, chopped
1 garlic clove, crushed
1/2 tsp turmeric
1/4 tsp chilli powder
450g/1lb parsnips, chopped
1.2 litres/2pts vegetable stock
Salt and pepper

Heat the oil in a saucepan and cook the onion for about 3 minutes until softened, then add the garlic, turmeric and chilli powder and cook for a further 1 minute. Add the parsnips and stir well.

Pour in the stock and bring to the boil, then cover and simmer for 15 minutes.

Allow the soup to cool, then transfer to a blender or food processor and purée until smooth. Transfer to a saucepan and reheat gently. Season to taste with salt and pepper before serving.

BROWN LENTIL SOUP

Serves 4

INGREDIENTS
1 onion, chopped
2 garlic cloves, crushed
2 celery sticks, chopped
2 tbsp olive oil
50g/2oz spaghetti, broken into small pieces
400g/14oz canned brown lentils, drained
1.2 litres/2pts vegetable stock
2 tbsp fresh mint, chopped

Place the onion, garlic and celery in a large frying pan with the oil and fry for 5 minutes. Add the spaghetti to the pan and stir to coat the pasta in the oil.

Add the lentils and stock and bring to the boil. Reduce the heat and simmer for 15 minutes, or until the pasta is tender. Remove the pan from the heat and stir in the mint. Serve immediately.

RED PEPPER SOUP

Serves 6

INGREDIENTS
4 red peppers, quartered and seeded
50ml/2fl oz vegetable oil
1 tsp dried mixed herbs
1 tsp mild curry paste
2 garlic cloves, crushed
1 red onion, sliced
250g/9oz green cabbage, chopped
4 tomatoes, skinned and chopped
1.2 litres/2pts water
1 tsp sweet chilli sauce
Salt and pepper

Place the peppers skin-side up under a hot grill until the skin blackens. Remove from the grill and allow to cool before peeling and chopping.

Heat the oil in a large pan and add the herbs, curry paste and garlic. Stir over a low heat for 1 minute. Add the onion and cook for 3 minutes. Add the cabbage, tomatoes, peppers and water and bring to the boil, then reduce the heat and simmer for 20 minutes. Remove from the heat and allow to cool slightly.

Place the soup in a blender or food processor and process until smooth. Return the soup to the heat and stir in the chilli sauce. Reheat and season to taste before serving.

BORSCHT

Serves 6

INGREDIENTS
1/2 red pepper, chopped
1 large cooking apple, chopped
1 onion, chopped
400g/14oz raw beetroot, peeled and chopped
3 celery stalks, chopped
100g/4oz mushrooms, chopped
25g/1oz butter
2 tbsp sunflower oil
2 litres/3 1/2pts vegetable stock
1 tsp cumin seeds

Place the pepper, apple, onion, beetroot, celery and mushrooms in a large saucepan with the butter, oil and 3 tbsp stock. Cover and cook gently for 15 minutes, stirring occasionally.

Stir in the cumin seeds, remaining stock and seasoning, then bring to the boil. Cover and reduce the heat to a gentle simmer and cook for about 30 minutes.

Strain the vegetables and reserve the liquid. Place the vegetables in a blender or food processor and process until they are smooth. Return them to the pan with the reserved liquid and reheat before serving.

ONION AND POTATO SOUP

Serves 12

INGREDIENTS
6 potatoes, cubed
6 onions, chopped
3 tbsp all-purpose flour
3 tbsp butter
1.2 litres/2pts milk
1 1/2 tbsp chopped fresh parsley
Salt and pepper

In a large pot over a high heat, combine the potatoes and onions with enough water to cover and boil for 30 to 45 minutes, or until tender. Drain the vegetables, reserving 600ml/1pt water. Transfer the vegetables to a blender or food processor in batches and purée until smooth.

In the same pot over a medium heat, combine the flour and butter. Slowly add the milk, stirring constantly, until well blended. Reduce the heat to low and add the potato and onion mixture. Simmer, stirring occasionally, for 5 to 10 minutes. Add the parsley and season to taste.

ARTICHOKE SOUP

Serves 4

INGREDIENTS
1 tbsp olive oil
1 garlic clove, crushed
1 onion, chopped
800g/1lb 12oz canned artichoke hearts, drained and chopped
600ml/1pt hot vegetable stock
150ml/¼pt single cream
2 tbsp fresh thyme, stalks removed

Heat the oil in a large saucepan and fry the garlic and onion until softened. Add the artichokes and stock, stir well, then bring to the boil. Reduce the heat and simmer, covered, for 3 minutes.

Transfer the mixture to a blender or food processor and purée until smooth, then pour into a large bowl. Stir in the cream and thyme, then cover and allow to cool. Place in the refrigerator for at least 6 hours. Serve chilled.

CELERIAC AND STILTON SOUP

Serves 6

INGREDIENTS
600g/1lb 5oz celeriac, peeled and cubed
1 onion, finely chopped
25g/1oz butter
1.2 litres/2pts vegetable stock
100g/4oz Stilton
150ml/¼pt single cream
Salt and pepper

In a large saucepan, sauté the celeriac and onion in the butter over a low heat until softened. Add the stock and bring to the boil. Reduce the heat, cover and simmer gently for 20 minutes.

Purée the soup in a blender or food processor, then return to the pan. Crumble in the Stilton and heat gently, stirring, until the Stilton melts. Stir in the cream and season to taste before serving.

TOMATO AND RICE SOUP

Serves 4

INGREDIENTS
400g/14oz canned chopped tomatoes
2 garlic cloves, crushed
Grated zest of 1/2 lime
1 tsp granulated sugar
2 tbsp olive oil
300ml/1/2pt hot vegetable stock
150g/5oz basmati rice
Salt and pepper

Place the tomatoes and their juice in a large saucepan with the garlic, lime zest, sugar and oil. Bring to the boil, then reduce the heat, and cover and simmer for 10 minutes.

Add the stock and rice and cook, uncovered, for a further 20 minutes. Season to taste and serve immediately.

LEEK AND POTATO SOUP

Serves 6

INGREDIENTS
50g/2oz butter
4 leeks, chopped
1/2 onion, chopped
2 potatoes, diced
900ml/1 1/2pts vegetable stock
150ml/1/4pt double cream
Salt and pepper

Melt the butter in a large saucepan, then add the leeks, onion and potatoes and stir well to combine over a medium-low heat. Cover and leave for 15 minutes.

Pour in the stock, then cover again and simmer for 20 minutes until the vegetables are tender.

Press the vegetables and stock through a sieve, then transfer to a clean pan and cook gently for 5 minutes. Stir in the cream and season to taste, then reheat gently before serving.

MOROCCAN CHICKPEA SOUP

Serves 6

INGREDIENTS
175g/6oz dried chickpeas
3 tbsp olive oil
1 onion, chopped
1 celery stalk, chopped
1 tsp ground cinnamon
450g/1lb tomatoes, skinned and chopped
100g/4oz lentils
1.2 litres/2pts vegetable stock
50g/2oz farfalle
Salt and pepper

Soak the chickpeas in a bowl of cold water overnight, then drain, rinse and set aside.

Heat the oil in a large saucepan and cook the onion and celery over a low heat until softened. Add the cinnamon and cook, stirring, for 2 minutes. Stir in the tomatoes and lentils and mix well. Add the chickpeas and cook gently for about 6 minutes.

Add the stock and simmer gently for about 1 1/2 hours, or until the chickpeas are tender.

Add the farfalle and simmer for a further 15 minutes. Season to taste and serve hot.

ORANGE AND PUMPKIN SOUP

Serves 4

INGREDIENTS
2 tbsp olive oil
2 onions, chopped
2 garlic cloves, chopped
900g/2lb pumpkin, peeled and cut into 2.5cm/1in chunks
1.2 litres/2pts hot vegetable stock
Grated zest and juice of 1 orange
2 tbsp fresh thyme, stalks removed
Salt and pepper
150ml/1/4pt milk

In a large saucepan heat the oil, then add the onions and cook for 4 minutes, until softened. Add the garlic and pumpkin and cook for a further 2 minutes, stirring well.

Add the stock, orange zest and juice and thyme and leave to simmer, covered, for 20 minutes. Transfer to a blender or food processor and purée until smooth. Season to taste.

Return the soup to the saucepan and add the milk. Reheat for 4 minutes but do not allow to boil.

STARTERS, PÂTÉS & DIPS

Whether you eat these dishes as starters or snacks, the most important thing is that you try them! Dips, blinis and dumplings are here, right next to pancakes and pastries. Not only would these recipes be perfect to begin a formal meal, but some of them would also make great party snacks, either to pass around with drinks at an adults' get-together, or as finger food for a child's birthday party.

YAM FRITTERS

Serves 5

INGREDIENTS
675g/1 1/2lb yams, peeled and cut into chunks
Salt and pepper
50ml/2fl oz milk
2 eggs, beaten
3 tbsp chopped tomato
3 tbsp chopped spring onion
1 green chilli, seeded and finely sliced
Salt and pepper
Plain flour, for shaping
50g/2oz fresh white breadcrumbs
Vegetable oil, for shallow-frying

In a large pan of salted water, boil the yams for 30 minutes until tender. Drain and mash with the milk and 3 tablespoons eggs. Add the tomato, spring onions, chilli and seasoning and mix thoroughly.

Shape the yam and vegetable mixture into round fritters about 7.5cm/3in in diameter with your hands.

Dip each fritter into the remaining beaten egg and then coat evenly with the breadcrumbs. Heat a little oil in a large frying pan and fry the fritters for about 5 minutes until golden brown on both sides. Drain well on kitchen paper before serving.

DUMPLINGS IN YOGURT

Serves 4

INGREDIENTS
200g/7oz urid dahl powder
1 tsp baking powder
1/2 tsp ground ginger
700ml/1 1/4pts water
Vegetable oil, for deep-frying

For the sauce:
400ml/14fl oz natural yogurt
400ml/14fl oz water
75g/3oz granulated sugar

Place the urid dahl powder, baking powder and ginger in a large bowl and stir to combine. Add the water and mix to form a batter.

Heat some oil in a deep saucepan. Pour in the batter, 1 teaspoon at a time, and deep-fry the dumplings until golden brown.

Place the yogurt in a separate bowl. Add the water and sugar and mix together with a whisk. Serve with the dumplings.

AVOCADO AND HERB DIP

Serves 4

INGREDIENTS
1 tbsp sour cream
1 avocado, chopped
1 tbsp lemon juice
1 tbsp olive oil
25g/1oz coriander leaves
1 tomato, peeled and chopped
Salt and pepper

Place the sour cream, avocado, lemon juice, oil, coriander and tomato into a blender or food processor and purée until smooth. Season with salt and pepper.

Transfer to a glass bowl and lay clingfilm directly on the surface of the dip to prevent a skin forming. Refrigerate the dip until ready to serve.

POTATO PANCAKES

Serves 6

INGREDIENTS
900g/2lb potatoes, grated
2 eggs
1 tbsp grated onion
50g/2oz self-raising flour
Pinch of grated nutmeg
Salt and pepper
Vegetable oil, for shallow-frying

Soak the potato in cold water for 1 1/2 hours, then drain well and pat dry with kitchen paper.

Beat together the eggs, onion, flour and nutmeg, then mix in the potato and season well.

Heat a thin layer of oil in a frying pan and drop a tablespoon of potato batter into the pan. Cook until golden brown and drain on kitchen paper and repeat with the remaining batter.

STUFFED PEPPERS

Serves 6

INGREDIENTS
6 red peppers
200g/7oz long-grain rice
4 tbsp olive oil
1 onion, finely chopped
3 tomatoes, diced
4 tbsp white wine
2 garlic cloves, finely chopped
100g/4oz Mozzarella cheese, diced
75g/3oz Parmesan cheese, grated
Salt and pepper

Preheat the oven to 190°C/375°F/Gas mark 5.

Slice the tops off the peppers and scoop out the seeds so they are hollow. Blanch them in boiling water for 4 minutes, then drain upside down.

Cook the rice following the packet instructions but drain and rinse in cold water 3 minutes before the end of the recommended cooking time.

Heat the oil in a frying pan and sauté the onion until soft. Stir in the tomatoes, wine and garlic and cook for 5 minutes. Remove from the heat, then stir in the rice and cheeses and season to taste.

Stuff the peppers with the rice mixture and arrange them in a shallow baking dish. Pour in enough water to come 1cm/1/2in up the sides of the peppers. Bake in the oven for 25 minutes, then serve immediately.

SUN-DRIED TOMATO BLINIS

Serves 6

INGREDIENTS
15g/¹/₂oz fresh yeast
350ml/12fl oz warm milk
2 eggs, separated
1 tsp caster sugar
100g/4oz buckwheat flour
100g/4oz strong white bread flour
1 tsp salt
2 tbsp sour cream
Butter, for frying
25g/1oz sun-dried tomatoes, sliced thinly

Crumble the yeast into the milk, add the egg yolks and sugar and stir well.

Sift the flours and the salt into a mixing bowl and make a well in the centre. Pour the milk mixture and sour cream into the well and mix. Cover and leave in a warm place for 1 hour, then whisk the egg whites until stiff, then fold into the batter.

Heat a small amount of butter in a frying pan and pour in 2 tablespoons of the batter, fry until both sides are set and golden brown. Cook the remaining blinis in the same way. Serve warm, topped with the sun-dried tomatoes.

AVOCADOS WITH CHEESE AND ONION

Serves 4

INGREDIENTS
1 tbsp vegetable oil
1 onion, sliced
1 garlic clove, crushed
1 tsp Worcestershire sauce
2 ripe avocados, halved and stoned
3 tomatoes, sliced
1 tbsp chopped fresh basil
75g/3oz Mozzarella cheese, sliced

Heat the oil in a frying pan and gently fry the onion and garlic until soft, then add the Worcestershire sauce.

Preheat the grill to medium-high and place the avocado halves on the grill pan.

Spoon the onions into the centre of the avocados, then divide the tomatoes and basil between the avocados. Finally, top each with the cheese. Grill until the cheese melts and starts to brown and serve hot.

SPICY GUACAMOLE

Serves 4

INGREDIENTS
2 avocados, peeled and stoned
3 tomatoes, peeled and finely chopped
5 spring onions, finely chopped
1 red chilli, seeded and finely chopped
2 tbsp lemon juice
Salt and pepper

Place the avocados into a large bowl and mash them with a fork. Add the tomatoes, spring onions, chilli and lemon juice.

Mix together well and season to taste.

MUSHROOM AND HERB PARCELS

Serves 4

INGREDIENTS
4 slices white bread, crusts removed
1 garlic clove, crushed
1 tsp Dijon mustard
75g/3oz chestnut mushrooms, sliced
150g/5oz oyster mushrooms, sliced
300ml/½pt vegetable stock
Salt and pepper
1 tbsp fresh chives, snipped

Preheat the oven to 180°C/350°F/Gas mark 4.

With a rolling pin, roll each slice of bread as thin as possible, then press each slice firmly into a 10cm/4in tartlet tin. Bake in the oven for 20 minutes.

Place the garlic, mustard, mushrooms and stock in a deep frying pan and stir-fry over a medium heat until the liquid is reduced by half.

Remove the mushrooms and set aside. Boil the remaining pan juices until reduced to a thick sauce and season well.

Stir the chives into the mushroom mixture and divide the mixture evenly between the bread cases. Spoon the pan juices over the parcels to serve.

MINI EGGS FLORENTINE

Serves 4

INGREDIENTS
8 slices white bread
2 tbsp olive oil
12 quail eggs
2 tsp lemon juice
100g/4oz butter
50g/2oz spinach, shredded

Preheat the oven to 180°C/350°F/Gas mark 4.

Cut 24 rounds from the bread with a 4cm/1 1/2in cutter. Brush both sides of the rounds with oil and bake for 15 minutes.

Add the quail eggs to a small pan of cold water and bring to the boil, stirring gently, and simmer for 4 minutes. Drain, then soak in cold water until cool. Peel, halve and remove the yolks, reserving the whites.

Process the yolks with the lemon juice in a blender or food processor for 10 seconds. With the motor running, add 75g/3oz butter and process until combined.

Melt the remaining butter in a pan, add the spinach and toss until just wilted. Divide evenly between the bread rounds, then top each round with half a quail egg and fill the cavity with the basil mixture.

PITTA BREAD

Serves 6

INGREDIENTS
2 tsp dry yeast
250ml/9fl oz warm water
350g/12oz plain flour
1 tsp salt

Dissolve the yeast in the water, then sift together the flour and salt and mix with the yeast and water. Work the mixture into a dough and knead for several minutes. Cover with a damp cloth and let rise in a warm place for 3 hours.

Preheat the oven to 180°C/350°F/Gas mark 4.

Divide the dough into 6 equal portions and roll into balls. With a rolling pin, pat and press each ball of dough into a 13cm/5in circle about 1cm/½in thick. Place on a baking tray and bake for 10 minutes or until light golden brown.

CHEESE PASTRIES

Serves 4

INGREDIENTS
225g/8oz butter, melted, plus extra for greasing
450g/1lb feta cheese, crumbled
2 eggs, beaten
6 tbsp Greek yogurt
16 sheets filo pastry

Preheat the oven to 200°C/400°F/Gas mark 6. Grease a baking
tray with butter.

In a large bowl combine the feta, eggs and yogurt, beating well
until smooth. Fit a piping bag with a 1cm/½in round nozzle and
spoon the cheese mixture into the bag.

Lay one sheet of pastry on to the work surface and fold it in half.
Brush with a little of the melted butter and pipe a line of the
cheese mixture along one long edge. Roll up the pastry to form a
sausage shape and brush with more melted butter. Repeat with
the remaining pastry and cheese mixture.

Arrange the pastries on the baking tray and bake for 20 minutes.
Cool on a wire rack before serving.

MUSHROOM BALLS

Serves 4

INGREDIENTS

Butter, for greasing
4 large flat mushrooms, stalks removed and chopped
25ml/1fl oz olive oil
Salt and pepper
1/2 onion, sliced
1 tsp cumin seeds
225g/8oz spinach, stalks trimmed, shredded
225g/8oz canned red kidney beans, drained
100g/4oz soft cheese

Preheat the oven to 190°C/375°F/Gas mark 5. Lightly grease a shallow ovenproof dish with butter.

Brush the mushrooms with some of the oil, then place them in the dish and season well. Cover with aluminium foil and bake for 20 minutes. Uncover, drain and reserve the juices.

Fry the onion and mushroom stalks in the remaining oil for 5 minutes. Then add the cumin seeds and mushroom juices and cook for a further 1 minute.

Stir in the spinach and fry until just wilted, then mix in the beans and heat well. Add the cheese, stirring until melted, and season again. Divide the mixture between the mushroom cups and return to the oven to heat through.

BHAJIS WITH YOGURT SAUCE

Serves 4

INGREDIENTS
175g/6oz gram flour, sifted
1 tsp bicarbonate of soda
1 tsp garam masala
1 1/2 tsp chilli powder
1 1/2 tsp turmeric
2 tbsp chopped fresh coriander
Salt and pepper
1 onion, sliced
1 leek, sliced
100g/4oz cooked cauliflower
Vegetable oil, for deep-frying

For the sauce:
150ml/1/4pt natural yogurt
2 tbsp chopped fresh mint
1/2 tsp turmeric
1 garlic clove, crushed

In a bowl, mix together the flour, bicarbonate of soda, garam masala, chilli powder, turmeric, coriander and seasoning.

Divide the mixture into 3 and place in separate bowls. Stir the onion into one bowl, the leek into another and the cauliflower into the third. Add 3 to 4 tablespoons water to each bowl and mix each to form a smooth paste.

Heat the oil in a deep saucepan until a cube of bread browns in 30 seconds. Using two forks, form the mixture into rounds and cook each in the oil for 4 minutes.

Remove with a slotted spoon and drain well on kitchen paper. Mix the sauce ingredients together and serve with the bhajis.

MUSHROOM CROÛTES

Serves 4

INGREDIENTS
For the croûtes:
Salt
1 litre/1 ¾pts water
175g/6oz polenta
25g/1oz butter
Olive oil, for frying

For the topping:
25g/1oz butter
2 shallots, finely chopped
450g/1lb button mushrooms, quartered
125ml/4fl oz Madeira
200ml/7fl oz whipping cream

To make the croûtes, bring the salted water to the boil in a large saucepan and slowly add the polenta, whisking constantly. Reduce the heat to a simmer and stir for 15 minutes. Stir in the butter and pour the mixture into an oiled container. Smooth the surface and set aside to cool.

When cold, cut the polenta into 12 rectangles, then fry each in olive oil on both sides until crisp. Drain on kitchen paper.

To making the topping, melt the butter and gently cook the shallots until soft and golden, then add the mushrooms and cook for a further 3 to 5 minutes. Add the Madeira and cook until the liquid evaporates. Stir in the cream and simmer until the sauce thickens. To serve, top the croûtes with the mushroom mixture.

PEPPER GRATIN

Serves 4

INGREDIENTS
2 tbsp olive oil
2 red peppers
4 tbsp fresh white breadcrumbs
8 black olives, stoned and roughly chopped
1 garlic clove, finely chopped
1 tbsp chopped fresh oregano
Salt and pepper

Preheat the oven to 200°C/400°F/Gas mark 6. Grease a small baking dish with a little of the oil.

Place the peppers under a hot grill, turning occasionally until they are blackened. Remove and leave to cool, then peel and chop into strips.

Arrange the peppers over the base of the baking dish then scatter the breadcrumbs, olives, garlic and oregano on top, seasoning to taste.

Bake in the oven for 20 minutes, then serve immediately.

EGG ROLLS

Serves 6

INGREDIENTS
Olive oil, for greasing and brushing
1 Chinese cabbage, outer leaves removed, shredded
2 carrots, shredded
2 garlic cloves, crushed
2 spring onions, chopped
1 tbsp finely chopped fresh ginger
1 tbsp soy sauce
2 tsp cornflour
1 tsp sesame oil
8 egg roll wrappers

Preheat the oven to 180°C/350°F/Gas mark 4. Grease a large
baking tray with olive oil.

Place the cabbage in a saucepan and cook over a medium heat
until just wilted, then transfer to a large bowl. Add the carrots,
garlic, spring onions, ginger, soy sauce, cornflour and oil and mix
well.

Arrange egg roll wrappers on a clean, dry surface. Spoon the
cabbage mixture diagonally on to each wrapper. Fold over one
corner to cover filling. Fold up both corners. Moisten edges of
remaining flap with water and roll up until sealed. Transfer egg
rolls to the prepared baking tray and brush with olive oil.
Bake in the oven for 25 minutes and serve hot.

AUBERGINE DIP

Serves 4

INGREDIENTS
4 pitta breads
2 large aubergines
1 garlic clove
1/4 tsp sesame oil
1/2 tsp ground cumin
1 tbsp lemon juice
Salt and pepper
2 tbsp chopped fresh parsley

Preheat the oven to 180°C/350°F/Gas mark 4.

Cut the pitta bread into strips and spread in a single layer on a baking tray. Cook in the oven for 15 minutes until golden and crisp, then leave to cool on a wire rack.

Heat a griddle pan, then cook the aubergines and garlic for about 15 minutes, turning the aubergines frequently.

When the aubergines are cool enough to handle, cut in half and scoop the flesh into a blender or food processor. Add the garlic and blend until smooth, then add the oil, cumin and lemon juice, then blend again to mix. Season to taste and stir in the parsley before serving.

HOT SOUR CHICKPEAS

Serves 4

INGREDIENTS

300g/11oz chickpeas, soaked overnight
4 tbsp vegetable oil
3 onions, very finely chopped
200g/7oz tomatoes, peeled and finely chopped
1 tbsp ground coriander
1 tbsp ground cumin
1 tsp ground cinnamon
1 tsp ground fenugreek
Salt
1 green chilli, seeded and finely sliced
2.5cm/1in piece fresh root ginger, peeled and grated
3 tbsp lemon juice

Drain the chickpeas and place them in a large saucepan, cover with water and bring to the boil. Cover and simmer for 1 to 1 1/2 hours until tender. Drain and reserve the cooking liquid.

Heat the oil in a large casserole dish. Reserve about 2 tablespoons of the onions and fry the remainder in the casserole dish over a medium heat for 5 minutes, stirring frequently.

Add the tomatoes and cook for a further 5 minutes, then mash into a pulp with the back of a spoon and stir well.

Mix in the coriander, cumin, cinnamon and fenugreek. Cook for 30 seconds and then add the chickpeas and 350ml/12fl oz of the reserved cooking liquid. Season with salt, cover and simmer for 20 minutes, stirring occasionally. Add more cooking liquid if it becomes too dry.

In a small bowl, mix together the reserved onion with the chilli, ginger and lemon juice. Shortly before serving, stir the chilli mixture into the chickpeas and adjust the seasoning to taste.

BRUSCHETTA

Serves 4

INGREDIENTS
50g/2oz sun-dried tomatoes
300ml/½pt boiling water
35cm/14in stick French bread, ends removed, cut into 12 slices
1 garlic clove, halved
25g/1oz black olives, stoned and quartered
2 tsp olive oil
2 tbsp chopped fresh basil
50g/2oz Mozzarella cheese, grated

Place the sun-dried tomatoes in a bowl, cover with the boiling water and set aside for 30 minutes. Drain well and pat dry with kitchen paper, then slice into thin strips and set aside.

Arrange the French bread slices on a grill rack and toast under a hot grill until lightly golden on each side.

Rub both sides of each slice with the cut sides of the garlic. Top with sun-dried tomato and olives.

Brush lightly with olive oil and sprinkle with the basil and cheese and return to the grill until the cheese has melted. Serve immediately.

GARLIC MUSHROOMS

Serves 4

INGREDIENTS
450g/1lb button mushrooms
3 tbsp olive oil
2 tbsp dry sherry
3 tbsp water
3 garlic cloves, crushed
100g/4oz soft cheese
3 tbsp chopped fresh chives
Salt and pepper
Toast, to serve

Place the mushrooms in a large saucepan with the oil, sherry and water and heat until bubbling, then cover and simmer for 5 minutes. Add the garlic and cook for a further 2 minutes, stirring.

Remove the mushrooms and set aside. Cook the liquid until it reduces down to 2 tablespoons. Remove from the heat and stir in the cheese and chives. Stir well until the cheese melts, then return the mushrooms to the pan and stir well. Reheat, season to taste and serve immediately on toast.

STUFFED CORNMEAL CHILLIES

Serves 6

INGREDIENTS
24 mild chillies
100g/4oz Cheddar cheese, grated
200g/7oz cream cheese
75g/3oz plain flour
4 eggs, lightly beaten
175g/6oz cornmeal
100g/4oz dry breadcrumbs
Vegetable oil, for deep-frying

Cut a slit down the length of one side of each chilli. Remove the seeds and membrane.

Combine the Cheddar and cream cheese and spoon some into each chilli. Put the flour on a large plate and the beaten egg in a small bowl. Combine the cornmeal and breadcrumbs on a flat dish.

Roll each chilli in the flour, dip in the egg and roll in the crumb mixture to coat thoroughly. Refrigerate for 1 hour. Repeat the dipping in egg and crumbs and refrigerate for a further 1 hour.

Fill a deep saucepan or a deep-fat fryer one-third full of oil and heat to 180°C/350°F or until a cube of bread browns in 30 seconds. Deep-fry the chillies in batches until golden brown. Remove with a slotted spoon and drain on kitchen paper before serving.

POTATO AND BEAN PÂTÉ

Serves 4

INGREDIENTS
100g/4oz potatoes, diced
75g/3oz canned borlotti beans, drained
150g/5oz canned kidney beans, drained
2 tsp lime juice
1 garlic clove, crushed
1 tbsp chopped fresh coriander
Salt and pepper
2 tbsp natural yogurt

Cook the potatoes in a saucepan of boiling water for 10 minutes until tender, then drain well and mash.

Transfer the potato to a blender and add the beans, lime juice, garlic and coriander. Season and purée until smooth.

Transfer to a bowl and stir in the yogurt. Refrigerate for 1 hour before serving.

SOURDOUGH BREAD

Serves 8

INGREDIENTS
50g/2oz fresh yeast
350ml/12fl oz water
225g/8oz plain flour
225g/8oz bread flour
3/4 tsp salt

Combine the yeast, water and plain flour in a large mixing bowl to make a thick batter and stir well, then set aside for at least 12 hours.

Add the bread flour to the batter and knead until the dough reaches a smooth, soft, moist consistency. Add more flour or water if necessary to achieve the proper consistency. After kneading for several minutes, add the salt and continue kneading until the dough forms a smooth, elastic, soft, moist ball.

Place the dough in a bowl and cover with clingfilm and leave to rise until it has doubled in volume.

Turn the dough out on to a well-floured surface and shape the dough into a ball. Allow the dough to rise until it is not quite fully proofed.

Preheat the oven to 230°C/450°F/Gas mark 8.

Bake the loaf for 40 minutes to 1 hour, or until well risen and golden. Leave to cool for at least 2 hours before serving.

STUFFED PEARS

Serves 4

INGREDIENTS
100g/4oz ricotta cheese
8 green olives, roughly chopped
4 dates, cut into thin strips
1 tbsp clear honey
1/2 celery stick, finely sliced
4 pears, halved and cored
150ml/1/4pt apple juice

Preheat the oven to 200°C/400°F/Gas mark 6.

Place the ricotta in a large bowl and add the olives, dates, honey and celery, then mix well.

Place the pear halves in a baking dish and divide the filling equally between them. Pour the apple juice into the dish, then cover with aluminium foil. Bake in the oven for 20 minutes. Remove and place under a hot grill for 3 minutes, then serve immediately.

SESAME PASTRY TWISTS

Serves 12

INGREDIENTS
Butter, for greasing
2 sheets puff pastry, thawed
1 egg, lightly beaten
75g/3oz sesame seeds

Preheat the oven to 200°C/400°F/Gas mark 6. Lightly grease 2 baking trays with butter.

Brush the pastry with the egg and sprinkle with sesame seeds.

Cut in half crossways and then into 1cm/½in wide strips. Twist the strips and place on the baking trays. Bake for 10 minutes, until golden, and serve immediately.

POTATO SKINS

Serves 4

INGREDIENTS
4 large baking potatoes
1 tbsp olive oil
1 tsp paprika
5 tbsp double cream
150g/5oz Cheddar cheese, grated
1 tbsp chopped fresh parsley

Preheat the oven to 200°C/400°F/Gas mark 6.

Scrub the potatoes, then prick them a few times with a fork and place directly on the top shelf of the oven. Bake for 1 hour, or until tender.

Set aside until cool enough to handle, then cut in half and scoop the flesh into a bowl and reserve. Preheat the grill and line the grill rack with aluminium foil.

Mix together the oil and paprika and use to brush the outside of the potato skins. Place on the grill rack and cook for 5 minutes until crisp.

Add the cream, cheese and parsley to the potato flesh and mix well. Halve the potato skins and fill with the cheese filling. Return to the oven for 15 minutes to heat through.

SPRING ROLLS

Serves 4

INGREDIENTS

25g/1oz fine cellophane noodles
2 tbsp groundnut oil, plus extra for deep-frying
1 garlic cloves, crushed
1/2 tsp grated fresh root ginger
75g/3oz mushrooms, thinly sliced
50g/2oz beansprouts
1 carrot, finely shredded
2 spring onions, finely chopped
1/2 tsp sesame oil
2 tbsp soy sauce
1 tbsp chopped fresh coriander
1 tbsp chopped fresh mint
24 spring roll wrappers
1/2 tsp cornflour

Place the noodles in a large bowl, pour over enough boiling water
to cover and leave to stand for 4 minutes. Drain, rinse in cold
water, then drain again. Cut the noodles into 5cm/2in lengths.

Heat the groundnut oil in a wok and add the garlic, ginger,
mushrooms, beansprouts, carrot and spring onions and stir-fry for
1 minute. Stir in the sesame oil, soy sauce, coriander and mint,
then remove the pan from the heat. Stir in the noodles.

Arrange the spring roll wrappers on a work surface. Mix the
cornflour with 1 tablespoon water to make a smooth paste and
brush the edges of a wrapper with it. Spoon a little filling on to the
wrapper.

Roll the point of the wrapper over the filling, then fold the side
points inwards over the filling. Continue to roll the wrapper away
from you, moistening the tip with a little more cornflour paste to
secure the roll. Repeat with the remaining wrappers and filling.

Heat the groundnut oil in a wok to 180°C/350°F, or until a cube of bread browns in 30 seconds. Add the spring rolls in batches and deep-fry for 3 minutes until golden and crisp. Drain on kitchen paper before serving.

DEEP-FRIED MOZZARELLA

Serves 4

INGREDIENTS
8 slices bread, crusts removed
100g/4oz Mozzarella cheese, sliced
75g/3oz black olives, quartered
16 basil leaves
Salt and pepper
150ml/1/4pt milk
4 eggs, beaten
Vegetable oil, for deep-frying

Cut each slice of bread into 2 triangles. Top half the triangles with equal amounts of Mozzarella and olives. Place the basil leaves on top and season well, then lay the other triangles of bread on top and press down around the edges to seal.

Mix the milk and eggs together and pour into an ovenproof dish. Add the sandwiches and leave to soak for about 5 minutes.

Heat the oil in a large saucepan until a cube of bread browns in 30 seconds. Carefully place the sandwiches in the oil and deep-fry in batches for 2 minutes or until golden, turning once. Remove with a slotted spoon and drain on kitchen paper before serving.

SALADS

Vegetables and salads are often wrongly dismissed as boring, plain meals – however, this section proves just how wrong that judgement is! Some people eat a vegetarian diet for health reasons or to lose weight, and for those people this section will provide meals that are interesting, healthy and meat-free. There are classics, such as the Waldorf salad and a vegetarian Caesar, and there are more unusual combinations, such as orange and tomato, or Italian tomato and bread. Some are more filling than others while some are best served as side dishes, but all are guaranteed to prove that salads should never be labelled boring!

NUT AND BEAN SALAD

Serves 6

INGREDIENTS
100g/4oz red kidney beans
50g/2oz white cannellini beans
Salt and pepper
2 tbsp olive oil
175g/6oz fresh green beans
3 spring onions, sliced
2 carrots, coarsely grated
1 green pepper, sliced
2 tbsp chopped sun-dried tomatoes
3 tbsp sunflower oil
2 tbsp red wine vinegar
1 tbsp coarse grain mustard
1 tsp caster sugar
1 tsp dried mixed herbs
50g/2oz unsalted cashew nuts

Soak the kidney and cannellini beans overnight, then drain and rinse well, cover with cold water and cook according to packet instructions. When cooked, drain and season the kidney and cannellini beans and toss them in the olive oil. Leave to cool for 40 minutes.

In a large bowl, mix in the green beans, spring onions, carrots, pepper and sun-dried tomatoes.

Make up the dressing by placing the sunflower oil, vinegar, mustard, sugar, herbs and seasoning in a screw-top jar and shaking well. Toss the dressing into the salad and add the cooked beans. Adjust the seasoning if necessary. Serve topped with the nuts.

ROAST RED PEPPER SALAD

Serves 4

INGREDIENTS
4 red peppers, halved and seeded
2 tbsp olive oil
150g/5oz unsalted cashew nuts

Preheat the oven to 200°C/400°F/Gas mark 6.

Place the pepper halves on a baking tray and roast for 20 to 30 minutes, until the skins are blackened and blistered.

When the peppers have cooled enough to handle, peel and chop the flesh into strips. Serve scattered with the nuts.

WALDORF SALAD

Serves 4

INGREDIENTS
4 green apples, cut into bite-size pieces
2 tbsp lemon juice
25g/1oz walnut pieces
5 celery sticks, sliced
250g/9oz mayonnaise
Salt and pepper

Place the apples in a large bowl, drizzle with the lemon juice and toss to coat. Mix in the walnut pieces and celery.

Add the mayonnaise and toss until well coated. Season to taste and serve.

BROAD BEAN SALAD

Serves 4

INGREDIENTS
350g/12oz broad beans
150ml/$\frac{1}{4}$pt natural yogurt
1 $\frac{1}{2}$ tsp lemon juice
1 tbsp chopped fresh mint
1 garlic clove, halved
Salt and pepper
1 red onion, thinly sliced
$\frac{1}{2}$ cucumber, peeled and sliced

Cook the broad beans in a small pan of boiling water until tender.
Drain, rinse under cold running water and drain again. Shell the
beans to leave only the sweet green beans.

Place the yogurt, lemon juice, mint, garlic and seasoning in a bowl
and stir well to combine.

Combine the onion, cucumber and beans. Toss them in the
dressing until well coated. Remove and discard the garlic and
serve immediately.

ITALIAN TOMATO AND BREAD SALAD

Serves 6

INGREDIENTS
4 thick slices day-old white bread
1 red onion, thinly sliced
100g/4oz Mozzarella cheese, thinly sliced
450g/1lb tomatoes, thinly sliced
1 tbsp shredded fresh basil
2 tbsp balsamic vinegar
150ml/¼pt extra virgin olive oil
Juice of 1 lemon
Salt and pepper

Dip the bread in cold water briefly, then carefully squeeze out any excess water and arrange the slices on the bottom of a shallow salad bowl. Soak the onions in cold water for 10 minutes, then drain.

Layer the onions, cheese, tomatoes and basil on top of the bread. Sprinkle with the vinegar, oil and lemon juice. Season to taste and refrigerate overnight before serving.

HOT POTATO SALAD

Serves 8

INGREDIENTS
2.7kg/3lb red potatoes
4 spring onions, sliced
3 tbsp chopped fresh parsley
Salt and pepper
175ml/6fl oz extra virgin olive oil
1 tbsp Dijon mustard
75ml/3fl oz white wine vinegar

Steam or boil the potatoes for 10 to 15 minutes, or until just
tender. Drain and cool slightly. Quarter the potatoes and place
in a bowl with the spring onion, parsley and season to taste.

To make the dressing whisk the oil, mustard and vinegar
together in a jug.

Pour half the dressing over the potatoes and toss to coat
thoroughly. Transfer to a serving bowl and drizzle with the
remaining dressing.

WARM LEEK SALAD

Serves 4

INGREDIENTS
675g/1 1/2lb leeks, trimmed and chopped
125ml/4fl oz olive oil
2 tbsp white wine vinegar
2 tsp Dijon mustard
1/2 tsp caster sugar
Salt and pepper
2 eggs, hard-boiled and chopped
100g/4oz pitted black olives
1 tbsp chopped fresh parsley

Cook the leeks in salted boiling water for 10 minutes until tender.
Drain well and dry on kitchen paper.

Make the dressing by mixing the oil and vinegar in a bowl, then
stirring in the mustard and sugar until smooth. Season well.

Arrange the leeks in a dish and pour the dressing over the top.
Sprinkle the eggs, olives and parsley over the leeks and serve
immediately.

GOATS' CHEESE SALAD

Serves 4

INGREDIENTS
1 tsp Dijon mustard
1 tsp dry white wine
1 tsp white wine vinegar
Salt and pepper
3 tbsp extra virgin olive oil
4 slices French bread
225g/8oz goats' cheese, cut into 4 slabs
175g/6oz mixed salad leaves

To make the dressing combine the mustard, wine and vinegar in
a large bowl. Season to taste, then whisk in the oil 1 tablespoon at
a time to form a thick vinaigrette.

Toast the bread on one side under a hot grill. Turn over the bread
and place a slab of cheese on each. Grill until the cheese is lightly
browned and bubbling.

Add the leaves to the salad bowl and toss to coat with the
dressing. Serve topped with the goats' cheese croutons.

SWEET AND SOUR ARTICHOKE SALAD

Serves 4

INGREDIENTS
6 small globe artichokes, outer leaves removed
Juice of 1 lemon
25ml/1fl oz olive oil
2 onions, roughly chopped
175g/6oz fresh broad beans, shelled
300ml/1/2pt boiling water
175g/6oz frozen peas
Salt and pepper
125ml/4fl oz white wine vinegar
1 tbsp caster sugar
Handful of mint leaves, torn

Cut the artichokes into quarters and place in a bowl. Add enough water to cover and then add the lemon juice.

Heat the oil in a large saucepan and add the onions. Fry until golden, then add the beans and stir. Drain the artichokes and add them to the pan. Pour in the boiling water and cook, covered, for 10 to 15 minutes.

Add the peas, season well and cook for a further 5 minutes, stirring occasionally. Strain the vegetables and place them in a bowl. When they are cool, cover and chill until ready to serve.

To make the sauce, combine the vinegar, sugar and mint leaves in a small pan and heat gently until the sugar dissolves. Simmer gently for about 5 minutes, stirring occasionally, then leave to cool. Drizzle over the vegetables to serve.

SWEET POTATO SALAD

Serves 4

INGREDIENTS
1 sweet potato, peeled and diced
2 carrots, sliced
100g/4oz canned chickpeas, drained
2 tomatoes, chopped
10 iceberg lettuce leaves
1 tbsp chopped walnuts
1 tbsp sultanas

Cook the sweet potato in a large pan of boiling water for 10 minutes. Add the carrots and cook for a further 4 minutes. Drain well and place in a bowl. Add the chickpeas and tomatoes and mix thoroughly.

Line a salad bowl with the lettuce leaves and spoon the vegetable mixture into the centre. Sprinkle with the walnuts and sultanas.

Spring rolls (see page 52)

Above, Pumpkin Pie (see page 110); Right, Caesar Salad (see page 75)

Above, Ricotta ravioli (see page 94); Below, Pasta with tomato salsa (see page 91)

Above, Feta spaghetti (see page 82); Right, Roast red pepper salad (see page 58)

Above, Noodles with mushroom sauce (see page 83); Below, Mushroom curry (see page 103)

Above, Tofu curry (see page 134); Right, Egg rolls (see page 43)

Above, Pepper omelette fingers (see page 101); Below, Vegetable stir-fry (see page 90)

Peanut soup (see page 15)

CABBAGE SALAD WITH PESTO DRESSING

Serves 4

INGREDIENTS

1 egg yolk
2 tsp lemon juice
200ml/7fl oz sunflower oil
Salt and pepper
2 tsp pesto
4 tbsp natural yogurt
1 small white cabbage, thinly sliced
3 spring onions, finely sliced
4 carrots, grated
25g/1oz pine nuts
1 tbsp chopped fresh mixed herbs

To make the dressing, place the egg yolk in a blender or food processor and process with the lemon juice. With the motor running, very slowly add the oil. Season to taste and add a little more lemon juice if necessary.

Spoon 75ml/3fl oz of the dressing into a bowl and stir in the pesto and yogurt, beating well.

Place the cabbage in a large salad bowl. Add the spring onions, carrots, pine nuts and herbs, and mix together thoroughly with your hands. Stir the dressing into the salad and serve.

ROASTED VEGETABLE SALAD

Serves 6

1 aubergine
2 red peppers
2 onions
2 courgettes
6 garlic cloves
6 tbsp olive oil
Salt and pepper
4 tomatoes
2 tbsp sherry vinegar
Juice of 1/2 lemon
2 tbsp chopped parsley

Preheat the oven to 180°C/350°F/Gas mark 4. Place the aubergine, peppers, onions, courgettes and garlic in a large roasting pan. Drizzle the oil over the top and season well, then bake in the oven for 30 to 40 minutes, adding the tomatoes after 15 minutes.

Allow the vegetables to cool slightly, then thickly slice and chop them and arrange them in a serving bowl.

Peel the garlic and mash the flesh into the pan juices. Mix in the vinegar and lemon juice, and pour the mixture over the roasted vegetables. Sprinkle with parsley to serve.

CAESAR SALAD

Serves 4

INGREDIENTS
1 garlic clove
3 tbsp sunflower oil
100g/4oz mushrooms, chopped
2 slices thick white crustless bread, cubed
1 cos lettuce, torn
50g/2oz Parmesan cheese, grated
2 eggs
2 tbsp extra virgin olive oil
2 tsp French mustard
2 tsp Worcestershire sauce
2 tbsp lemon juice

Preheat the oven to 190°C/375°F/Gas mark 5.

In a saucepan heat the garlic clove slowly in the sunflower oil and cook the mushrooms for 3 minutes. Remove the mushrooms and reserve. In the same pan toss in the bread cubes, mixing well to coat. Remove the garlic clove.

Spread the bread cubes on a baking tray and bake in the oven for 10 minutes. Remove and allow to cool.

Toss the lettuce, mushrooms and cheese together in a large salad bowl.

Boil a small saucepan of water and cook the eggs for 1 minute only. Remove the eggs and crack them open into a bowl. The whites should be milky and the yolks raw. Whisk the oil, mustard, Worcestershire sauce and lemon juice into the eggs to make the dressing. When ready to serve, pour the dressing over the leaves, toss well and serve topped with the bread cubes.

PASTA
&
GRAINS

Macaroni, spaghetti, linguine, lasagne – pasta can be cooked and prepared in so many different ways that we have filled an entire section of this book with main course recipes that centre around pastas and grains, such as couscous and rice.

Whether it is herb-filled ravioli, chilli pasta or vegetable paella, there is something here for everyone. These main courses may be slightly lighter than those in the main course section, making them ideal for warm summer evenings.

MACARONI AND POTATO BAKE

Serves 4

INGREDIENTS

475g/1lb 1oz dried macaroni
1 tbsp olive oil
4 tbsp butter, melted
450g/1lb potatoes, thinly sliced
450g/1lb onions, sliced
225g/8oz Mozzarella cheese, grated
Salt and pepper
150ml/¼pt double cream

Preheat the oven to 200°C/400°F/Gas mark 6.

Add the macaroni and oil to a saucepan of boiling water, then bring back to the boil and cook for about 12 minutes or until the pasta is just tender. Drain thoroughly.

Place the butter in a large casserole dish, then make alternate layers of potatoes, onions, macaroni and cheese in the casserole dish, seasoning well. Finish with a layer of cheese, then pour the double cream over the top.

Bake in the oven for 25 minutes, then brown the top under a hot grill and serve.

SPINACH AND RICOTTA SHELLS

Serves 4

INGREDIENTS
400g/14oz dried large pasta shells
75ml/3fl oz olive oil
125ml/4fl oz milk
50g/2oz fresh white breadcrumbs
300g/11oz frozen spinach, defrosted and drained
225g/8oz ricotta cheese
Pinch of freshly grated nutmeg
Salt and pepper
1 garlic clove, crushed
400g/14oz canned chopped tomatoes, drained

Preheat the oven to 180°C/350°F/Gas mark 4.

Bring a large saucepan of lightly salted water to the boil. Add the pasta and 1 tablespoon oil, bring back to the boil and cook for 8 to 10 minutes until just tender. Drain the pasta and set aside until required.

Place the milk, breadcrumbs and 3 tablespoons oil in a blender or food processor and blend to combine. Add the spinach and ricotta and process to a smooth mixture. Transfer to a bowl, stir in the nutmeg and season to taste.

Mix together the garlic, tomatoes and the remaining oil and spoon the mixture into the base of a large ovenproof dish.

Using a teaspoon, fill the pasta with the ricotta mixture and arrange them on top of the tomato mixture in the dish.

Cover and bake for 20 minutes. Serve hot.

MACARONI CHEESE

Serves 4

INGREDIENTS
450ml/3/4pt milk
300ml/1/2pt double cream
1 bay leaf
1/2 cinnamon stick
50g/2oz butter
2 tbsp plain flour
200g/7oz Cheddar cheese, grated
100g/4oz Parmesan cheese, grated
375g/13oz macaroni

Preheat the oven to 180°C/350°F/Gas mark 4.

Pour the milk and cream into a medium pan with the bay leaf and cinnamon stick. Bring to the boil, then remove from the heat and set aside for 10 minutes. Strain into a jug, then remove and discard the bay leaf and cinnamon stick.

Melt the butter in a medium pan over a low heat. Add the flour and stir for 1 minute. Remove from the heat and add the milk mixture gradually, stirring until smooth. Return to the heat and stir constantly until the sauce boils and thickens. Simmer for 2 minutes, then remove from the heat and add half the cheeses and season to taste. Set aside.

In a large pan of boiling salted water cook the macaroni until al dente. Drain and return to the pan. Add the sauce and mix well. Spoon into a deep casserole dish and sprinkle well with the remaining cheeses. Bake for 15 to 20 minutes and serve hot.

FETA SPAGHETTI

Serves 3

INGREDIENTS
100g/4oz spaghetti
Salt and pepper
1 garlic clove
2 tbsp extra virgin olive oil
8 cherry tomatoes, halved
1/2 green pepper, chopped
1/2 red pepper, chopped
100g/4oz fresh peas
75g/3oz feta cheese, crumbled
1 tbsp chopped fresh basil

Boil the spaghetti in lightly salted water according to packet instructions, then drain and set aside.

In the same pan, gently heat the garlic in the oil for 2 minutes, then add the tomatoes, peppers and peas. Increase the heat and fry the vegetables for 1 minute, then remove and discard the garlic.

Return the spaghetti to the pan and toss well, then stir in the feta and basil. Check the seasoning and serve hot.

NOODLES WITH MUSHROOM SAUCE

Serves 6

INGREDIENTS
350g/12oz dry spaghetti noodles
1 tbsp olive oil
15g/1/2oz butter
6 fresh mushrooms, sliced
1/2 garlic clove, crushed
Salt and pepper
125ml/4fl oz white wine
225ml/8fl oz vegetable stock
100g/4oz sour cream
15g/1/2oz cornflour

Bring a large pot of lightly salted water to a boil. Add the pasta and oil. Cook for 7 minutes, or until tender, then drain well.

Melt butter in a frying pan over a low heat. Add the mushrooms and cook until soft and dark. Stir in the garlic, seasoning, white wine and stock. Increase the heat to medium and cook, stirring constantly, for 5 minutes.

Reduce the heat to low, and stir in the sour cream until smooth. Stir in the cornflour and simmer for 1 minute to thicken. Serve the sauce spooned on top of the pasta.

VEGETABLE LASAGNE

Serves 4

INGREDIENTS
3 tbsp olive oil
2 garlic cloves, crushed
2 red onions, sliced
4 green peppers, diced
2 celery sticks, sliced
250g/9oz mushrooms, sliced
2 courgettes, diced
1/2 tsp chilli powder
1/2 tsp ground cumin
2 tomatoes, chopped
300ml/1/2pt passata
Salt and pepper
2 tbsp butter
1 tbsp plain flour
150ml/1/4pt vegetable stock
300ml/1/2pt milk
75g/3oz Cheddar cheese, grated
1 tsp Dijon mustard
1 egg, beaten
8 pre-cooked lasagne verdi sheets

Preheat the oven to 180°C/350°F/Gas mark 4.

Heat the oil in a pan and sauté the garlic and onion for 2 minutes. Add the peppers, celery, mushrooms and courgette and cook, stirring constantly, for 4 minutes. Stir in the spices and cook for a further 1 minute. Mix in the tomatoes and passata and season to taste.

For the cheese sauce, melt the butter in a pan, stir in the flour and cook for 1 minute. Remove from the heat and stir in the stock and milk. Return to the heat and boil, stirring for 3 minutes, or until thickened. Stir in half the cheese and all of the mustard. Remove from the heat, cool slightly and stir in the beaten egg.

Place half the lasagne sheets in an ovenproof dish. Top with half the vegetable mixture. Repeat the layers, then spoon the cheese sauce on top.

Sprinkle the lasagne with the remaining cheese and cook in the oven for 40 minutes, until the top is golden brown.

GARLIC TAGLIATELLE

Serves 4

INGREDIENTS
2 tbsp walnut oil
2 garlic cloves, thinly sliced
4 spring onions, sliced
200g/7oz mushrooms, sliced
450g/1lb fresh tagliatelle
250g/9oz frozen chopped spinach, thawed and drained
150g/5oz soft cheese with garlic and herbs
4 tbsp single cream
Salt and pepper
2 tbsp chopped fresh basil

Gently heat the oil in a wok or frying pan and fry the garlic and spring onions for 1 minute. Add the mushrooms, stir well, cover and cook gently for 5 minutes or until softened.

Bring a large saucepan of lightly salted water to the boil and cook the tagliatelle for 5 minutes until just tender. Drain thoroughly and return to the saucepan.

Add the spinach to the mushrooms and cook for 2 minutes. Add the cheese and allow to melt slightly. Stir in the cream and continue to heat without allowing to boil.

Pour the mixture over the pasta, season to taste and mix well. Heat gently, stirring, for 3 minutes. Place in a serving bowl and sprinkle with the basil before serving.

LEEK AND MUSHROOM RISOTTO

Serves 4

INGREDIENTS
2 tbsp olive oil
3 garlic cloves, crushed
250g/9oz mushrooms, roughly chopped
200g/7oz leeks, roughly chopped
Salt and pepper
75g/3oz butter
1 onion, roughly chopped
375g/13oz risotto rice
1.2 litres/2pts hot vegetable stock
Grated zest of 1 lemon
50g/2oz Parmesan cheese, grated
4 tbsp chopped fresh parsley

Heat the oil in a large saucepan and cook the garlic for 1 minute.
Add the mushrooms, leeks and seasoning and cook over a
medium heat for 10 minutes. Remove from the pan and set aside.

Add 25g/1oz butter to the pan and cook the onion for about 5
minutes until softened. Stir in the rice and cook for a further
1 minute.

Add a ladleful of stock and cook until the liquid has been
absorbed, stirring occasionally. Repeat until all the stock is
absorbed, this should take about 25 minutes.

Stir in the mushrooms, leeks , lemon zest, remaining butter and
half the Parmesan and parsley. Season to taste and serve
sprinkled with the remaining Parmesan and parsley.

THREE CHEESE TORTELLINI

Serves 6

INGREDIENTS
Butter, for greasing
450g/1lb fresh tortellini
2 eggs
350g/12oz ricotta cheese
Salt and pepper
25g/1oz fresh basil leaves
150g/5oz Cheddar cheese, grated
50g/2oz Parmesan cheese, grated

Preheat the oven to 190°C/375°F/Gas mark 5. Grease a baking dish with the butter.

Cook the tortellini in boiling salted water according to the package instructions and drain well.

Beat the eggs with the ricotta and season. Spoon half the tortellini into the baking dish, pour half the ricotta mixture over the top, then half the basil.

Sprinkle the Cheddar and remaining basil over, then top with the remaining tortellini, then the remaining ricotta mixture. Sprinkle the Parmesan evenly over the top and bake in the oven for about 40 minutes, until brown and bubbling.

SPICY NOODLES

Serves 4

INGREDIENTS
4 green chillies, deseeded and sliced
2 tbsp rice vinegar
500g/1lb 2oz dried medium egg noodles
50g/2oz beansprouts
3 tbsp sunflower oil
1 garlic clove, crushed
Salt
15g/½oz chives, cut into 2.5cm/1in pieces

Soak the chilli slices in the vinegar for 2 hours. Place the noodles in a bowl, cover with boiling water and soak for 10 minutes. Drain and set aside. Soak the beansprouts in cold water for 10 minutes then drain.

Heat the oil in a large wok, add the garlic and stir, then add the chillies and vinegar and stir-fry for 1 minute.

Add the beansprouts, stir and then add the noodles. Stir in salt to taste and add the chives. Using 2 spoons toss the noodles for 1 minute, until they are heated through. Serve immediately.

PESTO LINGUINE

Serves 6

INGREDIENTS
2 garlic cloves, chopped
75g/3oz fresh basil leaves
50g/2oz pine nuts, toasted
175ml/6fl oz olive oil
75g/3oz Parmesan cheese, grated
Salt and pepper
500g/1lb 2oz linguine

Finely chop the garlic, basil and pine nuts together in a blender or food processor. With the motor running, slowly add the oil until a smooth paste is formed. Transfer the mixture to a bowl, stir in the Parmesan and season to taste.

Cook the pasta in a large saucepan of salted boiling water until al dente. Drain and return to the pan. Toss the pesto through the pasta until well coated, then serve.

VEGETABLE COUSCOUS

Serves 4

INGREDIENTS
2 garlic cloves, crushed
1 onion, chopped
3 tbsp olive oil
1 red pepper, diced
1 aubergine, diced
2 courgettes, diced
1/2 tsp ground ginger
2 tsp ground cumin
1/2 tsp allspice
600ml/1pt passata
150ml/1/4pt vegetable stock
150g/5oz canned chickpeas, drained
50g/2oz dried apricots, sliced
200g/7oz couscous
Salt and pepper

Fry the garlic and onion in the olive oil in a deep saucepan until soft. Add the pepper, aubergine and courgettes and fry gently, stirring occasionally, for 5 minutes.

Stir in the ginger, cumin and allspice, then add the passata and stock and bring to the boil. Reduce the heat, stir in the chickpeas and apricots and simmer for 25 minutes.

Ten minutes before serving, put the couscous in a colander and place above the simmering vegetables.

Spoon the couscous on to individual serving plates and top with the cooked vegetables to serve.

PASTA OMELETTE

Serves 2

INGREDIENTS
5 tbsp olive oil
1 fennel bulb, thinly sliced
1 onion, chopped
150g/5oz potato, diced
1 garlic clove, chopped
4 eggs
2 tbsp chopped fresh parsley
Pinch of chilli powder
Salt and pepper
100g/4oz cooked spaghetti, cut into 2.5cm/1in lengths
2 tbsp stuffed green olives, halved

Heat half the oil in a heavy-based frying pan over a low heat. Add the fennel, onion and potato and cook, stirring occasionally, for 10 minutes. Stir in the garlic and cook for 1 minute. Remove the pan from the heat, transfer the vegetables to a plate and set aside.

Beat the eggs until they are frothy. Stir in the parsley and chilli powder, then season to taste.

Heat 1 tablespoon oil in a clean frying pan. Add half the egg mixture to the pan, then add the cooked vegetables, pasta and half the olives. Pour in the remaining egg mixture and cook until the sides begin to set.

Cook, shaking the pan occasionally, until the underside is a light golden brown colour. Remove the omelette from the pan and wipe the pan clean with kitchen paper.

Heat the remaining oil in the pan. Invert the omelette into the pan and cook until the other side is golden brown.

Serve the omelette garnished with the remaining olives.

PASTA WITH TOMATO SALSA

Serves 4

INGREDIENTS

7 tomatoes, peeled and diced
2 tbsp lemon juice
Grated zest and juice of 1/2 lime
2 shallots, finely chopped
2 garlic cloves, finely chopped
3 red chillies, seeded and finely chopped
1/2 green chilli, seeded and finely chopped
500g/1lb 2oz fresh frusilli pasta

Place the tomatoes in a small pan and add the lemon juice, lime zest and juice and stir well. Add the shallots, garlic and chillies. Bring to the boil and simmer gently for 5 to 10 minutes until the salsa has thickened slightly.

Meanwhile, bring a large pan of salted water to the boil and add the pasta. Simmer gently for 4 minutes or until the pasta is just tender.

Drain the pasta and rinse well. Top with the salsa and stir well before serving.

VEGETABLE CANNELLONI

Serves 4

INGREDIENTS
125ml/4fl oz olive oil
1 aubergine, diced
225g/8oz spinach
75g/3oz mushrooms, chopped
4 garlic cloves, crushed
1 tsp ground cumin
Salt and pepper
12 cannelloni tubes
1 tbsp vegetable oil
1 onion, chopped
800g/1lb 12oz canned chopped tomatoes
1 tsp caster sugar
75g/3oz Mozzarella, sliced

Preheat the oven to 190°C/375°F/Gas mark 5.

Heat the olive oil in a frying pan, add the aubergine and cook over a medium heat, stirring frequently, for 3 minutes.

Add the spinach, mushrooms, half the garlic and the cumin and reduce the heat. Season to taste and cook, stirring constantly, for 3 minutes. Spoon the mixture into the cannelloni tubes and place in a single layer in an ovenproof dish.

To make the sauce, heat the vegetable oil in a pan and cook the onion and remaining garlic for 1 minute. Add the tomatoes and sugar and bring to the boil. Reduce the heat and simmer for about 5 minutes. Spoon the sauce over the stuffed cannelloni tubes.

Arrange the Mozzarella on top of the sauce and cook in the oven for 30 minutes. Serve immediately.

CHILLI PASTA

Serves 6

INGREDIENTS
2 garlic cloves, finely chopped
2 red chillies
200ml/7fl oz dry white wine
500g/1lb 2oz passata
250g/9oz canned chopped tomatoes
2 tbsp tomato purée
400g/14oz dried gemelli
3 tbsp chopped fresh parsley

Put the garlic, chillies, white wine, passata, tomatoes and
tomato purée into a large saucepan and bring to the boil,
stirring occasionally. Reduce the heat, cover and simmer
while you cook the pasta.

Bring a large pan of salted water to the boil. Add the pasta and
bring back to the boil, then reduce the heat and simmer for 10
minutes, until al dente. Drain well and place in a large serving dish.

Remove the chillies from the sauce, then pour the sauce over the
pasta to serve.

RICOTTA RAVIOLI

Serves 4

INGREDIENTS
300g/11oz strong plain bread flour
Pinch of salt
3 eggs, beaten
1 tbsp olive oil
Plain flour, for dusting

For the filling:
225g/8oz ricotta cheese
2 tbsp pesto sauce
1 egg yolk
Salt and pepper

To serve:
50g/2oz butter, melted
100g/4oz Parmesan cheese, grated

To make the pasta, sift the flour and salt into a mixing bowl.
Make a well in the centre, add the eggs, then draw in the flour
and mix well. Add the oil and mix well with your hands until you
have a soft dough.

Knead the dough on a floured surface for 10 minutes until elastic,
then leave to rest for a further 10 minutes. Roll out the dough
until it is really thin, then leave for another 10 minutes to dry out.
To make the filling, mix all the ingredients together in a bowl. Cut
the dough into 2 large squares and cut each one into smaller
squares. Drop teaspoonfuls of filling into the small squares and
top with another pasta square, pressing gently around the edges
to seal.

Bring a large pan of salted water to the boil and drop in the
squares. Cook for about 5 minutes, until they rise to the surface,
then remove with a slotted spoon and drain well. Serve with
melted butter and Parmesan.

AUBERGINE AND MINT PENNE

Serves 4

INGREDIENTS
2 large aubergines, cut into short strips
Salt and pepper
50g/2oz walnuts
25g/1oz fresh mint
15g/1/2oz flat leaf parsley
50g/2oz Parmesan cheese, grated
2 garlic cloves, chopped
6 tbsp olive oil
450g/1lb dried penne

Layer the aubergine strips in a colander with salt and leave
to stand for 30 minutes, then rinse well and drain.

For the sauce, place the walnuts, mint, parsley, Parmesan and
garlic into a blender or food processor and blend until smooth.
With the motor still running, slowly add the oil. Season to taste.

Cook the penne following the packet instructions. When the
penne is nearly ready, add the aubergine and cook for 3 minutes,
then drain well and transfer to a bowl. Toss well with the sauce
and serve immediately.

HERB-FILLED RAVIOLI

Serves 4

300g/11oz plain flour
3 eggs, beaten
3 tbsp olive oil
Plain flour, for dusting
2 tbsp grated Parmesan cheese
250g/9oz ricotta
2 tsp chopped fresh chives
1 tbsp chopped fresh parsley
2 tsp chopped fresh basil
1 tsp chopped fresh thyme
Salt and pepper
175g/6oz butter, melted

Sift the flour into a bowl and make a well in the centre. Gradually mix in the eggs and oil. Turn out on to a lightly floured surface and knead until smooth. Cover with clingfilm and leave for 30 minutes. Mix the Parmesan, ricotta and herbs. Season well.

Divide the dough into four portions, two slightly larger, and cover with a cloth. Lightly flour a work surface and, using a floured rolling pin, roll out one portion from the centre to the edge.

When a well-shaped circle has formed, fold the dough in half and roll it out again. Continue this process seven or eight times to make a smooth circle of pasta about 5mm/1/4in thick. Roll this sheet quickly and smoothly to a thickness of 2.5mm/1/8in. Repeat to create 4 sheets of pasta, two slightly larger. Keep covered until ready to use.

Spread one of the smaller sheets out on a work surface and place heaped teaspoons of cheese and herb filling at 5cm/2in intervals. Brush a little water between the filling along the cutting lines. Place a larger pastry sheet on top and firmly press together along the cutting lines. Cut the ravioli and transfer to a lightly floured baking tray. Repeat with the remaining dough and filling.

Cook the ravioli in batches in a large pan of salted simmering water for 5 minutes, or until tender. Top with melted butter.

VEGETABLE PAELLA

Serves 6

INGREDIENTS
1 aubergine, cut into chunks
Salt and pepper
6 tbsp olive oil
1 onion, sliced
1 green pepper, sliced
1 red pepper, sliced
3 garlic cloves, crushed
2 tsp paprika
200g/7oz risotto rice
600ml/1pt vegetable stock
400g/14oz canned chopped tomatoes
Pinch saffron strands, steeped in 3 tbsp hot water
Salt and pepper
150g/5oz green beans
100g/4oz mushrooms, sliced
350g/12oz canned chickpeas

Sprinkle the aubergine with salt and leave to stand in a colander for 30 minutes, then rinse and dry.

In a large frying pan, heat the oil and fry the onion, peppers, garlic and aubergine, stirring occasionally, for 5 minutes. Sprinkle in the paprika and stir well.

Stir in the rice, pour in the stock and add the tomatoes, saffron and seasoning. Bring to the boil and simmer for 15 minutes, uncovered, stirring occasionally.

Stir in the beans, mushrooms, chickpeas and liquor. Cook for a further 10 minutes, then serve hot.

VEGETABLE STIR-FRY WITH PASTA

Serves 4

INGREDIENTS
400g/14oz pasta shells
1 tbsp olive oil
2 carrots, thinly sliced
100g/4oz baby corn cobs
3 tbsp peanut oil
2.5cm/1in piece fresh ginger root, thinly sliced
1 large onion, thinly sliced
1 garlic clove, thinly sliced
1 small red pepper, seeded and thinly sliced
1 small green pepper, seeded and thinly sliced
Salt

For the sauce:
1 tsp cornflour
2 tbsp water
3 tbsp soy sauce
3 tbsp dry sherry
1 tsp clear honey

Cook the pasta in boiling salted water and add the olive oil.
When the pasta is tender, drain, then return to the pan, cover
and keep warm.

Cook the carrots and baby corn in boiling salted water for 2
minutes. Drain and reserve.

Heat the peanut oil in a large frying pan over a medium heat. Add
the ginger and fry for 1 minute, then remove with a slotted spoon
and discard.

Add the onion, garlic and peppers and stir-fry over a medium
heat for 2 minutes. Add the carrots and baby corn cobs and stir-
fry for a further 2 minutes, then stir in the pasta.

To make the sauce, put the cornflour into a bowl and mix with the water to make a smooth paste. Stir in the soy sauce, sherry and honey.

Pour the sauce over the vegetables and pasta, stir well and cook for a further 2 minutes, stirring occasionally. Serve hot.

COCONUT RICE

Serves 4

2 tbsp vegetable oil
1 onion, chopped
1 garlic clove, crushed
2 red chillies, seeded and chopped
225g/8oz long-grain rice
600ml/1pt coconut milk

Heat the oil in a deep frying pan and gently fry the onion and garlic until golden. Add the chillies and fry for a further 3 minutes.

Stir in the rice and coconut milk and bring to the boil, then reduce the heat and simmer gently for 20 minutes, stirring occasionally, until the rice is tender.

Cover the pan and set aside to steam for 5 minutes before serving.

MAIN COURSES

For too long people thought that a vegetarian main course was the same as a meat main, with the meat removed – namely vegetables only. This is no longer the general opinion, but few realise the true range of vegetarian main courses. Here we have tried to fit in as many as we can, including curries, tarts, roulades, casseroles, flans and pies. Burrito and burger meat-free mains are no longer limited to potatoes and peas, these treats will tempt even the most committed meat-eater to consider giving it up!

MUSHROOM CURRY

Serves 4

INGREDIENTS
3 tbsp peanut oil
1 tsp chopped dried fenugreek
1 onion, finely chopped
2 tsp chopped garlic
1 tsp chopped fresh ginger
1 tomato, chopped
2 tbsp chopped fresh coriander leaves
1 tsp chilli powder
1 tsp ground turmeric
Salt and pepper
125ml/4fl oz hot water
375g/13oz button mushrooms
250g/9oz potatoes, diced
1/2 tsp garam masala

To serve:
Boiled basmati rice

Heat the oil in a saucepan, add the fenugreek, then the onion and fry until soft and golden. Stir in the garlic, ginger, tomatoes and coriander leaves and cook, stirring, for 2 minutes.

Add the chilli powder, turmeric, seasoning and water. Bring to the boil then stir in the mushrooms and potatoes. Cover and simmer, stirring occasionally, until potatoes are tender.

Sprinkle with the garam masala and serve with rice.

NUT ROAST

Serves 6

INGREDIENTS
2 tbsp olive oil
1 large onion, diced
300g/11oz mushrooms, finely chopped
2 garlic cloves, crushed
200g/7oz raw cashews
200g/7oz Brazil nuts
100g/4oz Cheddar cheese, grated
25g/1oz Parmesan cheese, grated
1 egg, lightly beaten
2 tbsp chopped fresh chives
75g/3oz fresh wholemeal breadcrumbs
Salt and pepper

Grease a 14 x 21cm/5¹/2x 8¹/2in loaf tin and line with greaseproof paper. Preheat the oven to 180°C/350°F/Gas mark 4.

Heat the oil in a frying pan. Add the onion, mushrooms and garlic and fry until soft, then leave to cool.

Process the nuts in a blender or food processor until they are finely chopped. In a large bowl, combine the mushroom mixture, nuts, Cheddar, Parmesan, egg, chives and breadcrumbs and season to taste.

Press the mixture into the loaf tin and bake in the oven for 45 minutes, or until firm. Leave to cool for 5 minutes before turning out and cutting into slices before serving.

TOMATO CURRY

Serves 4

INGREDIENTS

400g/14oz canned chopped tomatoes
1 tsp crushed garlic
1 tsp chilli powder
1 tsp finely chopped fresh ginger
1/2 tsp ground coriander
1/2 tsp ground cumin
4 tbsp vegetable oil
3 dried red chillies, deseeded and chopped
1/2 tsp onion seeds
1/2 tsp mustard seeds
1/2 tsp fenugreek seeds
Pinch of white cumin seeds
2 tbsp lemon juice

Blend together the tomatoes, garlic, chilli powder, ginger, coriander and cumin in a large mixing bowl.

Heat the oil in a saucepan. Add the chillies and seeds and stir-fry for 1 minute. Remove the pan from the heat.

Add the tomato mixture to the spicy oil mixture and return the pan to the heat. Stir-fry for about 3 minutes. Reduce the heat and continue to cook, half-covered with a lid, stirring frequently, for 10 minutes.

Sprinkle 1 tablespoon lemon juice over the curry. Taste and add the remaining lemon juice if required. Serve hot.

YAM AND APPLE CASSEROLE

Serves 6

INGREDIENTS
650g/1 1/4lb yams
125ml/4fl oz water
450g/1lb apples, peeled, cored and sliced
225ml/8fl oz apple juice
2 tbsp cornflour, mixed with 3 tbsp water to form a paste
125ml/4fl oz clear honey
100g/4oz breadcrumbs

Preheat the oven to 180°C/350°F/Gas mark 4.

Steam the yams in the water for 15 to 20 minutes, until tender, then peel and cut them in 1cm/1/2in thick slices. Layer the slices in a casserole dish, then lay the apple slices on top of the yams.

Bring the apple juice to the boil, then add the cornflour paste to the juice and stir until the sauce is clear and thickened, then add the honey. Spoon the sauce over the apples, then top with the breadcrumbs.

Bake in the oven for 1 hour, until the apples are tender.

CHEESE AND SPINACH FLAN

Serves 8

INGREDIENTS
225g/8oz plain flour, plus extra for dusting
100g/4oz butter
1/2 tsp paprika
1/2 tsp English mustard powder
Pinch of salt
150g/5oz Cheddar cheese, grated
4 tbsp cold water

450g/1lb frozen spinach
1 onion, finely chopped
Salt and pepper
Pinch of grated nutmeg
225g/8oz cottage cheese
3 eggs, 1 beaten
50g/2oz Parmesan cheese, grated
150ml/1/4pt single cream

Put the flour in a bowl and rub in the butter until the
mixture resembles fine breadcrumbs. Stir in the paprika,
mustard powder, salt and cheese. Add the cold water and
bind to form a dough. Knead until smooth, wrap and chill
for 30 minutes.

Preheat the oven to 200°C/400°F/Gas mark 6.

To make the filling, put the spinach and onion in a pan, cover and
cook gently until the spinach has thawed and the onion is tender.
Increase the heat and stir until the mixture is dry. Season with
salt, pepper and nutmeg. Spoon the spinach into a bowl and cool
slightly. Add the cottage cheese, the 2 unbeaten eggs, the
Parmesan and cream.

Cut one-third off the pastry and put it to one side for a lid. On a
lightly floured surface, roll out the remainder and use to line a
23cm/9in loose-based flan tin. Pour the filling into the pastry case.

Roll out the reserved pastry and cut into a lid, then lay it over the
flan, cutting holes in the surface. Press the edges together and
brush the lid with the beaten egg and bake for 35 to 40 minutes,
until golden brown. Can be served hot or cold.

IRISH COLCANNON

Serves 4

INGREDIENTS

900g/2lb potatoes, cut into chunks
200g/7oz green cabbage, shredded
25g/1oz butter
3 spring onions, chopped
Salt and pepper
4 large eggs
75g/3oz Cheddar cheese, grated

Preheat the oven to 190°C/375°F/Gas mark 5.

Boil the potatoes until just tender, then drain and mash well.
Lightly cook the cabbage until just tender but still crisp. Drain the
cabbage and mix into the potato with the butter and spring
onions, then season to taste.

Transfer the mixture to an ovenproof dish and make 4 holes in
the mixture. Crack an egg into each hole and season well. Bake in
the oven for 12 minutes and serve sprinkled with the cheese.

BUTTERNUT SQUASH STIR-FRY

Serves 4

INGREDIENTS

3 tbsp groundnut oil
900g/2lb butternut squash, peeled and cubed
2 garlic cloves, crushed
1 onion, sliced
1 tsp cumin seeds
2 tbsp chopped fresh coriander
150ml/1/4pt water
125ml/4fl oz coconut milk
100g/4oz salted cashew nuts

Heat the oil in a large wok and add the butternut squash, garlic and onion and stir-fry for 5 minutes. Stir in the cumin seeds and fresh coriander and stir-fry for a further 1 minute.

Add the water and coconut milk to the wok and bring to the boil. Cover and leave to simmer for 15 minutes until the squash is tender. Add the nuts and stir well. Serve immediately.

PEPPER OMELETTE FINGERS

Serves 2

INGREDIENTS
6 eggs
Salt and pepper
3 tbsp water
3 tbsp butter
1/4 red pepper, chopped
1/4 yellow pepper, chopped
1/2 green pepper, chopped.

In a medium-sized bowl, beat the eggs with a fork, then add seasoning and water and beat again.

In a frying pan, melt the butter over a medium heat. Pour eggs into heated pan. As eggs cook, lift up edges and tip pan to allow the uncooked egg on top to flow under the cooked eggs. Add in the peppers before the omelette sets.

The omelette is done when the bottom is browned and edges are set. Slide the omelette on to a plate and slice into fingers before serving.

PUMPKIN PIE

Serves 6

INGREDIENTS
Butter, for greasing
200g/7oz prepared sheet pastry
450g/1lb canned chopped pumpkin
25g/1oz granulated sugar
75g/3oz brown sugar
1 tsp ground cinnamon
1 tsp ground ginger
Pinch of salt
1 tsp ground cloves
175ml/6fl oz milk
3 eggs, lightly beaten
2 tsp vanilla essence

Preheat the oven to 190°C/375°F/Gas mark 5. Grease a 23cm/9in pie tin with butter. Fit the pastry into the tin.

Stir together the pumpkin, sugars, cinnamon, ginger, salt, cloves and milk until blended. Add the eggs and vanilla, stirring well, then pour the filling into the piecrust.

Bake in the oven for 50 minutes to 1 hour or until set in the centre. Cool completely on a wire rack before serving.

SPINACH ROULADE

Serves 4

INGREDIENTS

450g/1lb small fresh spinach leaves
2 tbsp water
4 eggs, separated
1/2 tsp ground nutmeg
Salt and pepper
175g/6oz small broccoli florets
25g/1oz Parmesan cheese, grated
175g/6oz Mozzarella cheese, grated

Preheat the oven to 220°C/425°F/Gas mark 7.

Wash the spinach and pack, still wet, into a large saucepan and add the water. Cover the pan with a tight-fitting lid and cook the spinach over a high heat for 4 minutes. Drain thoroughly, squeezing out any excess water, then pat dry and chop finely.

Mix the spinach with the egg yolks, nutmeg and season to taste. Whisk the egg whites until frothy and fold into the spinach mixture.

Grease a Swiss roll tin and line with greaseproof paper. Spread the mixture in the tin and smooth the surface. Bake in the oven for 15 minutes, until firm to the touch and golden.

Meanwhile, cook the broccoli in lightly salted boiling water for 5 minutes, until just tender.

Sprinkle the Parmesan on a sheet of baking parchment. Turn the spinach base on to it and peel away the lining paper. Sprinkle with the Mozzarella and top with the broccoli.

Hold one end of the paper and roll up the spinach base like a Swiss roll. Slice to serve.

CURRIED PARSNIP PIE

Serves 4

INGREDIENTS

For the pastry:
150g/5oz butter
225g/8oz plain flour
Salt and pepper
1 tsp dried oregano
8 shallots, peeled
3 carrots, thinly sliced
1 parsnip, thinly sliced
2 tbsp wholemeal flour
1 tbsp mild curry paste
300ml/1/2pt milk
150g/5oz Cheddar cheese, grated
2 tbsp chopped fresh parsley
1 egg yolk, beaten with 2 tsp water

Make the pastry by rubbing 100g/4oz butter into the plain flour until it resembles fine breadcrumbs. Season, then stir in the oregano, then mix in enough cold water to form a firm dough.

Blanch the shallots, carrots and parsnips for about 5 minutes. Drain and reserve 300ml/1/2pt of the liquid.

Melt the remaining butter in a clean pan and stir in the wholemeal flour and curry paste. Whisk in the reserved cooking liquid and milk and simmer for 2 minutes.

Remove the pan from the heat, stir in the cheese and seasoning, then mix in the vegetables and parsley. Pour the mixture into a pie dish with a pie funnel in the centre, and leave to cool.

Roll out the pastry large enough to fit the top of the pie dish and trim to fit. Lift on to the pie dish, making a hole for the funnel, seal well with your fingers around the edge. Brush all over with the egg wash.

Place the pie dish on a baking tray and chill for 30 minutes.

Preheat the oven to 200°C/400°F/Gas mark 6, then bake for 30 minutes.

TOMATO AND POTATO BAKE

Serves 6

INGREDIENTS
75ml/3fl oz olive oil, plus extra for brushing
2 large red onions, thinly sliced
475g/1lb 1oz tomatoes, thinly sliced
900g/2lb potatoes, thinly sliced
75g/3oz Parmesan cheese, grated
4 tbsp cold water
Salt and pepper

Preheat the oven to 180°C/350°F/Gas mark 4. Lightly grease a large baking dish with oil.

Arrange the onions in a layer in the dish, then a layer of tomatoes, followed by a layer of potatoes.

Pour the oil over and sprinkle the Parmesan over the top, then sprinkle the water over. Bake in the oven for 1 hour and serve hot.

CAULIFLOWER BAKE

Serves 4

INGREDIENTS

500g/1lb 2oz cauliflower, cut into florets
600g/1lb 5oz potatoes, cubed
25g/1oz butter
1 leek, sliced
1 garlic clove, crushed
3 tbsp plain flour
1/2 tsp paprika
300ml/1/2pt milk
50g/2oz Cheddar cheese, grated
3 tbsp chopped fresh parsley
100g/4oz cherry tomatoes
25g/1oz Parmesan cheese, grated

Preheat the oven to 180°C/350°F/Gas mark 4.

Cook the cauliflower in a saucepan of boiling water for 10 minutes. Meanwhile, cook the potato in a saucepan of boiling water for 10 minutes. Drain both and reserve.

Make the sauce by melting the butter in a large saucepan, then adding the leek and garlic and cooking for 1 minute over a low heat. Stir in the flour and cook, stirring constantly, for 1 minute. Remove the saucepan from the heat, then gradually stir in the paprika, milk, Cheddar and parsley. Return to the heat and bring to the boil, stirring constantly.

Transfer the cauliflower to an ovenproof dish with the cherry tomatoes, then top with the potatoes. Pour the sauce over the potatoes and sprinkle the Parmesan over the top.

Cook in the oven for 20 minutes, or until the vegetables are cooked through and the cheese is golden brown and bubbling. Serve immediately.

COURGETTE TART

Serves 4

INGREDIENTS
100g/4oz plain wholemeal flour
100g/4oz self-raising flour
Pinch of salt
100g/4oz butter, diced, plus extra for greasing
75ml/3fl oz iced water
1 tbsp sunflower oil
2 courgettes, sliced
1 garlic clove, crushed
150ml/1/4pt double cream
2 egg yolks
1 tbsp chopped fresh dill
Salt and pepper

Sift the flours and salt into a large bowl. With your fingertips rub in the butter until the mixture resembles fine breadcrumbs. Gradually add the iced water and knead until the mixture forms a dough, then wrap and chill for 30 minutes.

Preheat the oven to 200°C/400°F/Gas mark 6. Grease a 20cm/8in flan tin with butter.

Roll out the pastry and ease it into the flan tin. Prick the base and bake for 15 minutes, or until golden.

To make the filling, heat the oil in a frying pan and cook the courgettes until lightly browned. Mix the garlic, cream, egg yolks and dill in a bowl and season to taste.

Layer the courgettes in the pastry case and pour over the cream mixture. Bake for 30 minutes or until the filling is firm. Allow to cool in the tin before serving.

MIXED VEGETABLE CURRY

Serves 4

INGREDIENTS
6 tbsp vegetable oil
200g/7oz turnips, peeled and cubed
300g/11oz new potatoes
1 large onion, sliced
275g/10oz cauliflower, divided into florets
5cm/2in piece of fresh ginger, chopped
2 garlic cloves, crushed
2 green chillies, deseeded and chopped
1 tbsp paprika
1 tbsp mild curry powder
450ml/3/4pt vegetable stock
225g/8oz button mushrooms, sliced
400g/14oz canned chopped tomatoes
Salt and pepper
150ml/1/4pt coconut milk
1 tbsp cornflour
3 tbsp ground almonds

Heat the oil in a large saucepan, add the turnip, potatoes, onion and cauliflower and cook gently for 3 minutes, stirring frequently. Add the ginger, garlic, chillies, paprika and curry powder and cook for 1 minute, stirring.

Add the stock, mushrooms and tomatoes and season to taste. Cover and simmer gently for 35 minutes, stirring occasionally.

Blend the coconut milk and cornflour to make a smooth paste and stir into the mixture. Add the almonds and simmer for 2 minutes, stirring constantly. Taste and adjust the seasoning if necessary. Serve hot.

TOMATO AND ONION PIZZA

Serves 4

INGREDIENTS
Butter, for greasing
350g/12oz plain flour
15g/$\frac{1}{2}$oz easy blend yeast
2 tsp salt
1 tbsp olive oil
1 onion, chopped
$\frac{1}{2}$ garlic clove, crushed
1 red pepper, thinly sliced
250ml/9fl oz tomato purée
1 tbsp chopped fresh basil
175g/6oz Mozzarella cheese, grated
175g/6oz Cheddar cheese, grated

Preheat the oven to 220°C/425°F/Gas mark 7. Lightly grease a baking tray with butter.

Mix the flour, yeast and salt together, then mix to a firm dough with warm water.

Knead the dough for about 5 minutes until it is smooth and elastic then roll it out to a large circle and place on the baking tray. Leave to rise slightly while you make the topping.

Heat the oil in a frying pan and fry the onion and garlic over a moderate heat for 3 to 4 minutes until the onion is slightly softened. Add the pepper and continue cooking until the onion is lightly golden, stirring regularly.

Spread the base with the tomato purée. Add the onion and pepper. Scatter over the basil leaves and sprinkle with the cheeses.

Bake in the oven for 15 to 20 minutes, or until the crust is lightly browned. Allow to cool slightly before serving.

POTATO GNOCCHI

Serves 6

INGREDIENTS
1 tbsp olive oil
1 celery stick, chopped
1 onion, chopped
2 carrots, chopped
800g/1lb 12oz canned crushed tomatoes
1 tsp granulated sugar
Salt and pepper
25g/1oz butter
225g/8oz plain flour, plus extra for dusting
900g/2lb potatoes, mashed
2 eggs, beaten
75g/3oz Parmesan, grated

To make the sauce, heat the oil in a large frying pan, add the celery, onion and carrot and cook for 5 minutes, stirring regularly. Add the tomato and sugar and season to taste. Bring to the boil, reduce the heat to very low and simmer for 20 minutes. Cool slightly and process in batches in a blender or food processor until smooth.

To make the potato gnocchi, stir the butter and flour into the mashed potato using a wooden spoon, then beat in the eggs.

Turn the potato mixture on to a floured surface and divide into two. Roll each portion into a long sausage shape, then cut into short pieces and press each piece with the back of a fork.

Cook the gnocchi in batches in a large pan of boiling water for about 2 minutes, or until the gnocchi rise to the surface. Using a slotted spoon, drain the gnocchi and transfer to serving bowls and serve with the sauce. Sprinkle with the grated Parmesan and serve immediately.

ROAST BUTTERNUT SQUASH

Serves 4

INGREDIENTS

2 small butternut squash
1 tbsp olive oil
3 garlic cloves, crushed
Salt and pepper
1 tbsp walnut oil
3 leeks, trimmed and thinly sliced
1 tbsp black mustard seeds
350g/12oz canned cannellini beans, drained and rinsed
75g/3oz fine French beans, halved
150ml/1/4pt vegetable stock
1 tbsp freshly snipped chives
75g/3oz rocket
4 tbsp fromage frais

Preheat the oven to 200°C/400°F/Gas mark 6.

Cut the butternut squash in half lengthways and scoop out all of
the seeds. Score the squash in a diamond pattern with a sharp
knife. Mix the olive oil with the garlic and brush over the cut
surfaces of the squash. Season well with salt and pepper. Put on a
baking tray and roast for 40 minutes until tender.

Heat the walnut oil in a saucepan and fry the leeks and mustard
seeds for 5 minutes. Add the beans and stock. Bring to the boil
and simmer gently for 5 minutes.

Remove from the heat and stir in the chives and rocket. Season
well. Remove the squash from the oven and allow to cool for 5
minutes. Spoon in the bean mixture and serve immediately with
the fromage frais.

BEETROOT ROULADE

Serves 6

INGREDIENTS
225g/8oz fresh beetroot, cooked, peeled and roughly chopped
1/2 tsp ground cumin
25g/1oz butter
4 eggs, separated
2 tsp grated onion
Salt and pepper
150ml/1/4pt double cream
1/2 tsp dry mustard powder
2 tsp white wine vinegar
3 tbsp chopped fresh dill
3 tbsp horseradish relish
1 tsp granulated sugar
2 tbsp chopped fresh parsley

Preheat the oven to 190°C/375°F/Gas mark 5. Line a Swiss roll tin
with greaseproof paper.

In a blender or food processor, purée the beetroot. Then beat in
the cumin, butter, egg yolks, onion and seasoning. Place the
beetroot mixture into a large bowl.

In a separate bowl, whisk the egg whites until they form stiff
peaks, then fold them carefully into the beetroot mixture.

Spoon the mixture into the Swiss roll tin, then level and bake for
15 minutes. Leave to cool on a wire rack.

Beat the cream until lightly stiff, then fold in the mustard powder,
vinegar, dill, horseradish, sugar and parsley. Spread the mixture
on to the beetroot and roll up. Cut into slices and serve.

VEGETABLE BAKE

Serves 4

INGREDIENTS
1 tbsp olive oil
675g/1 1/2lb potatoes, thinly sliced
8 fresh basil leaves
2 leeks, sliced
2 beef tomatoes, thinly sliced
1 garlic clove, finely chopped
300ml/1/2pt vegetable stock
Salt and pepper

Preheat the oven to 180°C/350°F/Gas mark 4.

Brush a large ovenproof dish with a little of the oil. Place a layer of potato slices in the base, sprinkle with half the basil leaves and cover with a layer of leeks. Arrange the tomatoes in a layer on the top. Repeat these layers until all the vegetables are used up, ending with a layer of potatoes.

Stir the garlic into the stock and season to taste. Pour the stock over the vegetables and brush the top with the remaining oil.

Bake in the oven for 1 1/2 hours until the vegetables are tender and the topping is golden brown.

VEGETABLE STIR-FRY

Serves 6

INGREDIENTS
4 tbsp soy sauce
1/2 tsp grated palm sugar
50ml/2fl oz vegetable stock
2 tbsp vegetable oil
3 garlic cloves, crushed
4 spring onions, cut into 3cm/1 1/4in lengths
1 red chilli, seeded and sliced
75g/3oz button mushrooms, quartered
100g/4oz Chinese cabbage, roughly chopped
150g/5oz broccoli, cut into small florets
100g/4oz mangetout
200g/7oz cauliflower, cut into small florets

Combine the soy sauce with the palm sugar and stock in a small
bowl. Heat a wok over a high heat, add the oil and swirl to coat.
Add the garlic, spring onion and chilli and stir-fry for 20 seconds.

Add the mushrooms and Chinese cabbage and stir-fry for 1
minute. Stir in the sauce, broccoli, mangetout and cauliflower.
Cook for 2 minutes, or until tender. Serve hot.

CAULIFLOWER CHEESE

Serves 4

INGREDIENTS

500g/1lb 2oz cauliflower, cut into small pieces
25g/1oz butter, plus extra for greasing
25g/1oz plain flour
1 tsp Dijon mustard
300ml/½pt warm milk
50g/2oz Parmesan cheese, grated
75g/3oz Cheddar cheese, grated
Salt and pepper
2 tbsp fresh breadcrumbs

Lightly grease a 1.2 litre/2pt heatproof dish.

Cook the cauliflower pieces in a saucepan of lightly salted boiling
water for 10 minutes, or until just tender. Drain thoroughly, then
transfer to the prepared dish and keep warm.

For the cheese sauce, melt the butter in a pan over a low heat.
Stir in the flour and cook for 1 minute, or until pale and
foaming. Remove from the heat and gradually stir in the
mustard and milk. Return to the heat and stir constantly until
the sauce boils and thickens. Reduce the heat and simmer for 2
minutes, then remove the pan from the heat. Add the Parmesan
and 50g/2oz Cheddar and stir until melted. Season to taste and
pour over the cauliflower.

Combine the breadcrumbs and remaining Cheddar and sprinkle
over the sauce. Grill under a medium heat until the top is brown
and bubbling. Serve immediately.

LENTIL CRÊPES

Serves 6

INGREDIENTS
100g/4oz plain flour
1 egg
300ml/1/2pt buttermilk
Salt and pepper
1 fennel bulb, thinly sliced
2 leeks, thinly sliced
4 tbsp olive oil
175g/6oz red lentils
150ml/1/4pt dry white wine
400g/14oz canned chopped tomatoes
300ml/1/2pt vegetable stock
1 tsp dried oregano
200g/7oz mushrooms, sliced
1 onion, sliced
250g/9oz frozen leaf spinach, thawed
200g/7oz cream cheese
75g/3oz Parmesan cheese, grated

Make the pancake batter by mixing the flour, egg, buttermilk and
a pinch of salt in a blender or food processor until smooth.

To make the filling, gently fry the fennel and leeks in half the olive
oil for 5 minutes, then add the lentils and wine. Cook for a further 1
minute until reduced down, then stir in the tomatoes and stock.

Bring the leek mixture to a boil, add the oregano and seasoning
then simmer for 20 minutes, stirring occasionally.

Preheat the oven to 190°C/350°F/Gas mark 5. Lightly grease a
20cm/8in round deep spring-form cake tin.

Fry the mushrooms and onion in the remaining olive oil for 5
minutes, stir in the spinach and heat through. Season well, then
mix in the cream cheese.

In a frying pan make 12 pancakes with the batter, then use some of the pancakes to line the prepared cake tin, overlapping to cover fully.

Layer the remaining pancakes with the two fillings, sprinkling Parmesan between the layers and pressing them down well. Finish with a pancake on top.

Cover with foil and set aside to rest. Bake in the oven for 40 minutes, then turn out and leave for 10 minutes before serving.

POTATO AND LEEK PIE

Serves 8

INGREDIENTS
Salt and pepper
800g/1 3/4lb new potatoes, thinly sliced
75g/3oz butter
400g/14oz leeks, sliced
Salt and pepper
25g/1oz fresh parsley, finely chopped
4 tbsp chopped mixed herbs
12 sheets filo pastry
150g/5oz Cheddar cheese, sliced
2 garlic cloves, finely chopped
250ml/9fl oz double cream
2 large egg yolks

Preheat the oven to 190°C/375°F/Gas mark 5.

Bring a pan of lightly salted water to the boil and cook the potatoes for 4 minutes, then drain.

Melt 25g/1oz butter in a frying pan and cook the leeks gently, stirring occasionally, until softened. Remove from the heat, season to taste, then stir in half the parsley and half the mixed herbs.

Melt the remaining butter. Line a 23cm/9in round loose-based cake tin with 7 filo sheets, brushing each layer with butter. Let the edges of the pastry overhang the tin.

Layer the potatoes, leeks and cheese in the tin, sprinkling herbs and garlic between the layers. Flip the overhanging pastry over the filling and cover with 2 sheets of filo, tucking in the sides and brushing with melted butter. Cover the pie loosely with foil and bake for 35 minutes.

Beat the cream, egg yolks and remaining herbs together. Make a hole in the centre of the pie and gradually pour in the mixture. Arrange the remaining filo on top of the pie and brush with butter. Reduce the oven temperature to 180°C/350°F/Gas mark 4 and bake the pie for 25 minutes. Leave to cool before serving.

LEEK, TOFU AND POTATO PIE

Serves 4

1 leek, chopped
50g/2oz butter
1 garlic clove, crushed
50ml/2fl oz milk
900g/2lb potatoes
275g/10oz tofu, mashed
Juice of 1/2 lemon
Salt and pepper
500g/1lb 2oz puff pastry
1 egg, lightly beaten

Preheat the oven to 200°C/400°F/Gas mark 6.

Sauté the leek in the butter with the garlic until soft.

Mix the milk, mashed potatoes, tofu, leeks, lemon juice and seasoning in a bowl, then pile the mixture into a pie plate.

Roll the puff pastry between two sheets of baking paper so it fits over the filling in the pie plate. Brush the pastry with the egg and bake the pie for 20 to 30 minutes.

COURGETTE QUICHE

Serves 6

INGREDIENTS
100g/4oz wholemeal flour
100g/4oz plain flour
100g/4oz butter
3 tbsp cold water
1 red onion, thinly sliced
2 tbsp olive oil
2 courgettes, sliced
175g/6oz goats' cheese, grated
2 tbsp chopped fresh basil
3 eggs, beaten
300ml/½pt milk
Salt and pepper

Preheat the oven for 200°C/400°F/Gas mark 6.

Mix the flours together and rub in the butter until the mixture resembles fine breadcrumbs, then mix to a firm dough with the water. Roll out the pastry and use to line a 23cm/9in flan tin. Prick the base and chill for 30 minutes, then fill with greaseproof paper and baking beans. Bake blind on a baking tray for 20 minutes, uncovering it for the final 5 minutes.

Cook the onion in the oil for 5 minutes, until it is soft. Add the courgettes and fry for a further 5 minutes.

Spoon the onion and courgettes into the pastry case. Scatter over 150g/5oz cheese and the basil. Beat together the eggs, milk and seasoning and pour over the filling. Top with the remaining cheese.

Turn the oven down to 180°C/350°F/Gas mark 4 and return the quiche to the oven for about 40 minutes, until risen and firm to the touch in the centre. Allow to cool slightly before serving.

VEGETABLE CHILLI

Serves 4

INGREDIENTS
15g/1/2oz olive oil
1 red onion, finely chopped
2 red peppers, finely chopped
4 garlic cloves, crushed
800g/1lb 12oz canned chopped tomatoes
1/2 tsp ground cumin
1 tbsp mild chilli powder
1/2 tsp dried oregano
Salt and pepper
2 courgettes, sliced
400g/14oz canned kidney beans, drained and rinsed
450ml/3/4pt water
1 tbsp tomato purée
150g/5oz Cheddar cheese, grated

Heat the oil in a large saucepan over a medium heat. Add the onion and peppers and cook, stirring occasionally, for 4 minutes, or until the onion is softened. Add the garlic and cook for a further 3 minutes.

Add the tomatoes, cumin, chilli powder and oregano to the saucepan, then season to taste. Bring to the boil, reduce the heat, cover and simmer for 15 minutes.

Add the courgettes and kidney beans. Stir in the water and tomato purée. Return to the boil, then cover the saucepan and simmer for a further 45 minutes, or until the vegetables are tender. Taste and adjust the seasoning if necessary. Ladle into serving bowls and top with the cheese.

CHEESE AND TOMATO PIZZA

Serves 4

INGREDIENTS
400g/14oz canned chopped tomatoes
2 tsp dried basil
2 garlic cloves, crushed
1 tbsp olive oil
$1/2$ tsp granulated sugar
15g/$1/2$oz fresh yeast
6 tbsp hand-hot water
1 tbsp olive oil
175g/6oz plain flour
1 tsp salt
2 tbsp tomato purée
25g/1oz Parmesan cheese, grated
100g/4oz Mozzarella cheese, diced

To make the topping, place the tomatoes, basil, garlic and oil in a large heavy-based frying pan. Simmer the mixture over a low heat for 20 minutes or until the sauce has thickened. Stir in the tomato purée, remove the pan from the heat and leave to cool slightly.

Mix together the sugar, yeast and 4 tablespoons water. Leave in a warm place for 15 minutes or until frothy.

Sift together the flour and salt and make a well in the centre. Add the oil, yeast mixture and remaining water. Mix to form a smooth dough. Turn the dough out on to a floured surface and knead for 5 minutes or until smooth.

Return the dough to the bowl, cover with an oiled sheet of clingfilm and leave to rise for 30 minutes or until doubled in size.

Knead the dough for 2 minutes. Stretch the dough with your hands, then place it on an oiled baking tray, pushing out the edges until it forms an even circle. It should be no more than 5mm/$1/4$in thick as it will rise during cooking.

129

Preheat the oven to 200°C/400°F/Gas mark 6.

Spread the tomato topping evenly over the pizza base. Top with the cheeses and bake in the oven for 20 to 25 minutes. Serve hot.

BEAN SPROUT STIR-FRY

Serves 4

INGREDIENTS
2 tbsp sunflower oil
225g/8oz mixed sprouted beans
2 spring onions, chopped
2 tbsp chopped fresh parsley
1 garlic clove, crushed
1 tbsp sesame seeds
2 tbsp soy sauce
2 tsp sesame oil
Salt and pepper

Heat the oil in a large wok and stir-fry the sprouted beans, onion and garlic for 5 minutes.

Add the spring onions, parsley, garlic, sesame seeds, soy sauce and sesame oil and cook for a further 2 minutes. Season to taste and serve piping hot.

COURGETTE BURGERS

Serves 4

INGREDIENTS
300g/11oz courgettes, grated
1 onion, finely chopped
25g/1oz self-raising flour
50g/2oz Parmesan cheese, grated
1 tbsp chopped fresh mint
2 tsp chopped fresh parsley
Pinch of ground nutmeg
25g/1oz dry breadcrumbs
1 egg, lightly beaten
Salt and pepper
Olive oil, for shallow-frying

Put the courgettes and onion in the centre of a clean tea towel, gather the corners together and twist as tightly as possible to remove all the juices. Combine the courgettes, onion, flour, cheese, mint, parsley, nutmeg, breadcrumbs and egg in a large bowl. Season well then mix with your hands to a stiff mixture.

Heat the oil in a large frying pan over a medium heat. When hot, drop level tablespoons of mixture into the pan and shallow-fry for 3 minutes, or until well browned all over. Drain well on kitchen paper and serve hot.

POTATO CURRY

Serves 4

INGREDIENTS
3 potatoes, peeled and each cut into 6 slices
150ml/1/4pt vegetable oil
1/2 tsp fennel seeds
1 tsp onion seeds
4 curry leaves
1 tsp ground cumin
1/2 tsp turmeric
1 tsp ground coriander
1 tsp chilli powder
1 tsp salt
1 1/2 tsp dried mango powder

Cook the potato slices in a saucepan of boiling water until they are just cooked. Drain well and set aside.

Heat the oil in a separate saucepan over a medium heat. Reduce the heat and add the fennel seeds, onion seeds and curry leaves and stir thoroughly.

Remove the pan from the heat and add the ground cumin, turmeric, coriander, chilli powder, salt and dried mango powder, stirring well to combine.

Return the pan to a low heat and fry the mixture, stirring constantly, for about 1 minute. Pour the mixture over the cooked potatoes, mix together and stir over a low heat for about 5 minutes. Serve immediately.

LENTIL SHEPHERD'S PIE

Serves 4

INGREDIENTS
Butter, for greasing
2 tbsp vegetable oil
1 garlic clove, crushed
2 onions, chopped
2 tbsp plain flour
350ml/12fl oz vegetable stock
1/4 tsp dried thyme
Salt and pepper
400g/14oz canned brown lentils
275g/10oz frozen mixed vegetables
400g/14oz potatoes, mashed

Preheat the oven to 180°C/350°F/Gas mark 4. Lightly grease a casserole dish with butter.

In a medium saucepan, heat the oil and add the garlic and onions. Cook, stirring, for about 2 minutes or until softened, then stir in the flour until absorbed.

Add the stock, thyme, salt and pepper and cook, stirring, until the mixture comes to a boil. Stir in the lentils and vegetables and spoon the mixture into the casserole dish.

Spread the potatoes over the top of the lentil mixture, leaving a hole in the centre so steam can escape.

Bake in the oven for 40 minutes or until the potatoes are browned on top.

TOFU CURRY

Serves 4

INGREDIENTS
400g/14oz tofu, cubed
3 tbsp soy sauce
2 green chillies, seeded and chopped
2 garlic cloves, chopped
1 onion, chopped
1 tsp grated fresh ginger
Grated zest and juice of 1 lime
3 tbsp chopped fresh coriander
1 tsp granulated sugar
25g/1oz creamed coconut, dissolved in 150ml/$\frac{1}{4}$pt boiling water
2 tbsp groundnut oil

To serve:
Boiled rice

Toss the tofu in 2 tablespoons soy sauce and leave to marinate for 15 minutes.

Place the chillies, garlic, onion, ginger, lime zest and juice, coriander, the remaining soy sauce, sugar, coconut and water into a blender or food processor and pulse until smooth.

Heat the oil in a wok until hot, then drain the tofu and stir-fry until browned on all sides. Drain on kitchen paper and wipe out the wok.

Pour the contents of the blender or food processor into the wok and stir, return the tofu to the wok and reheat, stirring well. Serve with rice.

CHICKPEA BURRITOS

Serves 4

INGREDIENTS
Butter, for greasing
1 tbsp vegetable oil
2 onions, chopped
1 green pepper, chopped
1 garlic clove, crushed
1 red chilli, seeded and chopped
200g/7oz canned chopped tomatoes
1 tbsp tomato purée
400g/14oz canned chickpeas, drained
Salt and pepper
8 flour tortillas
4 spring onions, finely chopped
250g/9oz Cheddar cheese, grated

Preheat the oven to 180°C/350°F/Gas mark 4. Grease an ovenproof baking dish with butter.

Heat the oil and fry the onions until soft, then add the pepper and garlic and fry for a further 4 minutes. Stir in the chilli, tomatoes, tomato purée and chickpeas, then simmer for 10 minutes and season to taste.

Divide the mixture between the tortillas and sprinkle with the spring onions and 175g/6oz Cheddar. Fold the sides of each tortilla around the filling and secure with a cocktail stick, then place the burritos in the baking dish. Cover the dish with aluminium foil and bake in the oven for 15 minutes.

Sprinkle with the remaining Cheddar and place the burritos under the grill until the cheese is bubbling, then serve immediately.

Weights and Measures

Imperial	Metric	Imperial	Metric
1oz	25g	1³/₄lb	850g
2oz	50g	2lb	900g
3oz	75g	2¹/₂lb	1.1kg
4oz	100g	3lb	1.4kg
5oz	150g	3¹/₂lb	1.6kg
6oz	175g	4lb	1.8kg
7oz	200g	4¹/₂lb	2kg
8oz	225g	5lb	2.3kg
9oz	250g	5¹/₂lb	2.5kg
10oz	275g	6lb	2.7kg
11oz	300g	6¹/₂lb	3kg
12oz	350g	7lb	3.2kg
13oz	375g	7¹/₂lb	3.4kg
14oz	400g	8lb	3.6kg
15oz	425g	8¹/₂lb	3.9kg
16oz (1lb)	450g	9lb	4.1kg
1lb 2oz	500g	9¹/₂lb	4.3kg
1¹/₄lb	600g	10lb	4.5kg
1¹/₂lb	700g		

Imperial	Metric	Imperial	Metric
1fl oz	25ml	9fl oz	250ml
2fl oz	50ml	10fl oz (¹/₂pt)	300ml
3fl oz	75ml	12fl oz	350ml
3¹/₂fl oz	100ml	15fl oz (³/₄pt)	450ml
4fl oz	125ml	18 fl oz	500ml
5fl oz (¹/₄pt)	150ml	20fl oz (1pt)	600ml
6fl oz	175ml	30fl oz (1¹/₂pt)	900ml
7fl oz	200ml	35 fl oz (2pt)	1.2 litres
8fl oz	225ml	40 fl oz (2¹/₂pt)	1.5 litres

All the measurements given are for level spoonfuls (British Imperial
Standard). 1 teaspoon = 5ml, 1 tablespoon = 15ml